It's Time to Come Home

*With Kindness and Compassion,
We Come Back to Ourselves*

Stewart Blackburn

It's Time to Come Home:

With Kindness and Compassion, We Come Back to Ourselves

© 2018 by Stewart Blackburn.

All rights reserved.

Printed in the United States of America. No part of this book may be used or reproduced in any manner whatsoever without permission except in the case of brief quotations embodied in critical articles and reviews.

Fragrant House Publishing

12-7002 Lahela St.

Pahoa, HI 96778

FIRST EDITION

ISBN-13: 978-1721000050
ISBN-10: 1721000054

Dedication

This book is dedicated to the people and the ʻaina of lower Puna.

Table of Contents

Acknowledgments	vii
Introduction	ix
Chapter 1 – That Wondrous Feeling of Home	1
Meditation 1 – Desire	14
Chapter 2 – Calls to Come Home	17
Meditation 2 – Savoring Myself	31
Chapter 3 – Outfitting Ourselves for Our Trek Home	34
Meditation 3 – Self-Love	48
Chapter 4 – We Come Home to Feel Good	51
Meditation 4 – Helping My Body Heal	64
Chapter 5 – Getting Lost in Criticism	67
Meditation 5 – I Love Feeling Peaceful	80
Chapter 6 – Managing Expectation	83
Meditation 6 – Putting Childhood to Rest	94
Chapter 7 – The Past Needs Kindness, Too	97
Meditation 7 – It's Safe to Be Who I Am	110
Chapter 8 – The Stories That Make Us: Talking to Ourselves	112
Meditation 8 – Taking Up My Power	124
Chapter 9 – I Accept My Power	126
Meditation 9 – I Am Comfortable with My Sexuality	140
Chapter 10 – My Body Is My Faithful Friend	142
Meditation 10 – I Want My Body to Be Happy	157
Chapter 11 – Calling Every Part of Us to Come Home	161
Meditation 11 – Befriending Myself	173
Chapter 12 – Sharing the Peace	176
Dear Reader	189

Acknowledgments

I am deeply indebted to the brilliant work of Dr. Serge Kahili King. His investigations into the mechanics of feelings had a great influence on my thinking. His wisdom, mentorship, and most of all his friendship have helped to guide my explorations of the inner worlds. Thank you from the depths of my heart!

I want to thank the many people connected with the Kalani Honua Retreat Center, now sadly closed. It is through the programs I was able to teach there that I worked through many of the ideas and exercises presented in this book. Their assistance was invaluable and I am extremely grateful for it.

There have been many people who have contributed to this publication and I am grateful to all of you. I want to give a shout out especially to Tracy Matfin, Moîses Nascimento, Paul Blackburn, Gloria King, Lucy and John Pincence, Tritia Hamilton, Florian Walzenegger, Sylvie Chladek, Heidi Dew, Dr. Martin Schmidt, Ivonne Magin, and Omri Navot. Many thanks for your thoughts and support. Julie W. at Freelancer did a wonderful job of working with me to edit the first edition of this book. I am profoundly grateful for her fine work.

And a special thank you to my friend Lynn Thompson, the host of Living On Purpose, for all the loving work she did in polishing this book to make it even better! Mahalo nui loa!

I long, as does every human being, to be at home wherever I find myself.

Maya Angelou

Introduction

This book is about taking the noble but challenging road back to our own authenticity. It attempts to point the way through and past many of the pitfalls, detours, quagmires, seemingly insurmountable mountains, and wide, raging rivers that we encounter on that journey. There are many temptations and urges to deal with and far more advice than we could ever use. There will be well-meaning people who will encourage us to abandon this project for more "realistic" endeavors. And perhaps there will be others who want us to take them with us and lead them along our path.

Whatever the obstacles may be, there is no more significant journey in life than that of coming home to our real, authentic selves. It is the quintessential expedition into the unknown that also has the very highest treasure at the end—our true self.

But what's most curious is that all of the trials and complications are of our own doing. We are the ones who have made our own lives difficult. We have done this through the thoughts we hold each day, and the ideas that we base our choices on that probably don't serve us at all well.

Throughout this book I intend to point out, from my perspective, many of the ways we unintentionally hurt ourselves and that keep us wandering around in the dark looking for home. This is by no means a complete examination of the ways that we mistreat ourselves, or how we can stop doing so. But, by just acknowledging that we can do better, we start to open ourselves to the many things that can help us to make this change.

Coming home is a process that rewards every single bit of our effort. Each time we alter our pattern of self-abuse, we claim a little more of the self-love that is our birthright. And the more we treat ourselves with love, kindness, and compassion, the more we add those qualities to the world.

It's Time to Come Home

This book is divided into 12 chapters that look at different aspects of this journey. Between each chapter is a meditation that is included to provide ways of thinking about the different subjects. They are written in the first person to help you feel its meaning as you are reading. They are even more powerful when you can listen to them in a comfortable, relaxing space.

These meditations have been recorded and are posted on the Stewart Blackburn YouTube channel *It's Time to Come Home* playlist: (https://www.youtube.com/watch?v=OgTezsIVkJQ&list=PLs4PbR 01ICaa8f8SoWi4fvayw8xjHBiHK).

But recording them for yourself and listening to your own voice is even more powerful. The most useful way of working with them is just to feel what comes up as you listen to them or read them. All of this work is about feelings, and these meditations are just another way to stimulate them.

Jumping around and reading what appeals to you at any time is encouraged. While there is a logical sequence to the chapters, what's more important is your authority in choosing what's important for you at any given moment.

On a more personal note, the last two and a half months of working on this book have been of enormous challenge for me. I live in the area called lower Puna on the side of Kilauea volcano, on the Big Island of Hawaii. After a magnitude 6.9 earthquake, Kilauea has been erupting furiously all around me. All but one of the roads are closed, most of my neighbors have left, and the air quality is dangerous at times.

But it's been a powerful time for me to test the principles and techniques that I am presenting here. Trusting myself, keeping my vibration just as high as possible, and relaxing into intensity are my daily practices in this situation. I am now even more convinced of the value and power of this work.

If nothing else, please take away the essential message of this book—treat yourself with kindness and compassion in all you do. This simple act can change you and the world around you in profound ways. I wish you great peace and joy all the days of your life!

Find the love you seek, by first finding the love within yourself.
Learn to rest in that place within you that is your true home.
Sri Sri Ravi Shankar

Chapter 1

That Wondrous Feeling of Home

Home, by any definition, is a place where we feel we belong. As Dorothy Gale said, "There's no place like home." Home is where it is safe to be who we are, to let go of masks and pretense, and to feel the tranquility and peace that belongs to all of us. It is a sacred space that nurtures us when we most need it, and it lets us feel good inside no matter what.

As I watch the people all around me profoundly hurt themselves each day with their self-judgments, criticisms, and complaints, I am moved to say, "Hold it right there! You're just fine the way you are! You don't have to do *anything* to be lovable and valued." There are enormous pressures from all around us that would have us believe that if only we would do this, that, or the other, we will be "fixed" and everything will finally be alright. Perhaps to some extent they're right. However, without the element of personal compassion and a genuine kindness towards ourselves, nothing can or ever will be different. It is through kindness and compassion that we come home to ourselves.

I use the metaphor of home to name that inner space where we feel safe and loved. The experience of being at home, both in a physical place and in our inner world, is so delicious, nurturing, and soul-satisfying that it is a wonder that we don't demand more of it every day, especially that inner experience of being comfortably at home in our skin.

Why would we ever avoid being at home within ourselves? It's an important question that flies in the face of everything we know about "reality." Everywhere we look we can see people whose faces reveal varying levels of misery and unhappiness, even though they are perpetually struggling to feel good. Why aren't their efforts paying off? Why aren't they all just as happy as they'd like to be?

First. let's remember that the motivation to do *anything* is to feel better than we currently do. This is simply saying that the incentives for each action, the inspirations for each goal, and the criteria for each plan are always about what we imagine will make us feel as good as possible. That's what pleasure is. It is from this awareness that we can then see what's going on.

I use the word "pleasure" here as a catchall word to encompass the many ways that we can feel good. Pleasure is the response we have to a wide variety of experiences that we enjoy. We don't have another word that so thoroughly embraces this wide range of feelings that are so closely related. Pleasure is much more than the sexual feelings with which that word is so often associated. It is the rainbow of personal events that delight and invigorate us. It is the foundation upon which we build our lives. All the experiences that matter deeply to us—love, peace, joy, contentment, relaxation, and harmony—can be felt as pleasure. Every single decision that we make is based upon a quick calculation of what will likely give us the most pleasure (minus whatever pain is involved).

Unfortunately, many of our decisions don't lead us to feeling pleasure. In fact, they don't make us feel nearly as good as we were hoping for. We may buy a fancy car to attract lovers only to find that it's way too expensive and doesn't make up for any unpleasant personal features we might have. Or we may choose to live a particular lifestyle to find spiritual satisfaction but discover that our chosen path doesn't go where we thought it would. The point is that we are always trying to feel better, to find pleasure, but it is worth paying attention to what the payoffs for our efforts actually are.

Coming home is about a broad set of pleasures that all focus on feeling genuinely wonderful. In the best of circumstances, there is a sense of peace and acceptance at home. Home is the center of one's life, from which all endeavors and adventures start. There is a strong sense of safety and well-being connected to the concept of home. It's where we ache to be when we tire of work and the ceaseless striving for more in life. Even just saying the word "home" brings a little respite from the stresses of the day.

When we are at home the familiarity of our surroundings allows us to put our attention on the things that we enjoy without having to figure out any other details. We don't have to doubt ourselves about where things ought to be; where they have been living for years is just fine. Most of the little problems of existence have been solved, at least for now. Home is where we can relax in the broadest possible ways and not be questioned. When we're at home, we don't have to pretend to be other than who we are. We can take off our masks and breathe freely. It feels good to unwind and just be ourselves here.

This sense of peace and safety applies to our inner world as well as the more physical one. When we are at home within ourselves, we can dream unreservedly. Our imaginations can race out in all directions, and our most profound desires can be examined without judgment. There is a kind of freedom not felt anywhere else, where we are free to explore the deepest parts of ourselves, to let those desires and hurts rise to the surface and bask in the sunlight of awareness. Being at home within is more than being in a particular place or a specific state of mind. We feel good *about ourselves* when we are at home.

Feeling good about ourselves is in many ways the master feeling. It is the primary feeling that we strive to have as often as we possibly can. We get this feeling when we have accomplished essential tasks, fallen in love, and when we feel connected to the Divine in some way. While any particular experience of feeling at home may be subtler than these, whatever feeling is evoked is of the same nature.

On the other hand, when we don't feel good about ourselves we slide into depression, that belief that we aren't worthy of love, or anything else, and that life is hopeless. When we allow ourselves to slip into thoughts and feelings of worthlessness or any "less than" mentality, we have stumbled out of our home and are wandering about, cold and lost. When we allow ourselves to disapprove of some aspects of who we are, we take up the veil of shame and mistreat ourselves mercilessly. We think that rebuking ourselves will motivate us to be better people.

I'm sorry, but that just doesn't work. It doesn't work because, while it is motivated by the desire to feel better, it makes us feel bad about ourselves instead. The whole process lacks a basic compassion towards oneself. What is called for is a way of understanding how to treat ourselves that allows us to feel good about ourselves as we navigate the world. Kindness and compassion are the keys to this endeavor.

Another way of looking at compassion is that it is a feeling of wanting things to be much better than they are. It is a desire for more pleasure, in the broadest sense of the word, for others and for ourselves. Compassion happens when we view the world, other people, or anything from a place apart from our regular operating pattern, with our hearts open. We witness, with both our intellect and our emotions, what is happening from a slightly detached point of view that lets us see it from a wider perspective. When we take such a view of ourselves, we can be aware of both our experience and how we feel about that experience.

We seem to believe that the opposite of compassion will make our lives better. Consider how often we say unkind things to ourselves, like "that was dumb!" "my bad!" or "what a fool I've been!" Then there are the ways that we compare ourselves to others, generally unfavorably. We question whether or not we're *normal*. It's a feeling that we're not the way we should be and not who we should be. And this not-rightness creates stress in us. It eats away at our self-confidence and undermines our self-esteem to the point where we search in vain to find what will truly satisfy our sense of wholeness and belonging. This is the search for home.

Coming home is the process of accepting who we are in our entirety. It is the recognition that we are both different from others, with different skills, desires, and pleasures, and that we share a common physical and emotional foundation upon which we build our lives. It is the acknowledgment that while we seem to know a great many things, we don't know everything. In fact, what we know is quite limited considering how much there is to know. This means that we are always in the position of learning things. How do I do this? How can I handle that? What happens when I don't do what others say to do?

We are learning what it means to be individuals who are essential parts of everything. That seems contradictory, but we're talking about two different levels that exist simultaneously. It's like the fingers on our hand. Each finger has its own functions and skills. Each has its own specific needs and desires. They each have different experiences, albeit similar to the other fingers. Yet they are all parts of the greater whole. They are essential elements of the hand, as well as the arm, and the whole body. As such they are indispensable tools for the well-being of an entire person.

So while any given finger has a limited role, that role is vital. In the same way, each of us contributes whatever it is that makes us who we are to the fabric of the Universe. Yes, we may be single drops in the ocean. But that doesn't make us insignificant. Our particular creaturehood is meaningful in the way that every flower, slightly different from the others, makes the bouquet brighter and more beautiful. Each note in a symphony is vital to the harmony. Every shingle on the roof is essential to keeping water out of the house. We all have our parts to play and we all share in the glory of existence.

There's an interesting phenomenon in nature where pushing to make something work better, faster, more efficiently, or more powerfully makes it less so. For instance, adding too much fertilizer can cause the plant to grow too quickly and be more vulnerable to wind and rain. Pushing water through a pipe too hard can disrupt the smooth flow and not as much water can move through the pipe. Adding too much flavor to a dish like beef stew can overwhelm the mouth, and the stew actually tastes less flavorful. One perceives more flavor by adding water to dilute it.

This condition happens with humans, too. We try too hard to please someone else and end up pushing that person away. We work so hard to make money to enjoy ourselves on our time off that we're too exhausted to do anything after we finish working for the day. We eat so much good food that we make ourselves sick. And we make such a significant effort to be as close to perfection as possible, that we become miserable at our failure to be as perfect as we think we should be.

Where do these ideas come from? Why do we believe that we need to do more, that our endeavors are never enough, and that we can only think of ourselves in a good way when we have sacrificed as much as is humanly possible? At a basic level, of course, these notions are tied to what we thought had to be done to barter for love. "If I can be perfect, I will be loved."

It's a bargain that a lot of us have bought into. And it's such a habit to think like this that we seldom check to see if it actually works. Is there any relationship between how good I am and how loved I am? If I *never* disappoint anyone, will I be loved even more?

I wish someone would do a study on the effectiveness of the various beliefs in the world about how best to be loved. We can buy and try a lot of different ones, but we don't have a rating system for how well they work. Some have been so popular that they might be regarded as classics, like being nice and polite to others. There are more faddish beliefs, like being politically correct or brutally honest. There are some that are no longer popular, but they might make a comeback, like not speaking until one is spoken to or being exceptionally "pure" or "virtuous."

It's the belief that "being perfect is important" that I find so damaging. It is a belief that presupposes that one is not perfect the way one already is. We can never actually get to perfection, and thus we are always judging ourselves as less than perfect. In other words, we can never be good enough to be totally loved. How very, very sad!

So what beliefs might we adopt that would work better for us? The first one we might try on is the notion that *We're not here on Earth to win goodness points or gold stars for how well we behaved during our lives.* If

Heaven is the place after death where all the "good" people go, I think I would rather go elsewhere where I might find more interesting and adventurous companions.

Here's another belief that might fit: *I genuinely try to make the wisest decision I can at any given moment.* Oh sure, I may look back and realize that a decision didn't work out as well as I would have liked it to, but at the time I thought that the decision I made was a good choice. So, in essence, I'm doing the best I can all the time. Why, then, should I berate myself for not doing better? How could I have done better? I was doing the best I knew how to at that time.

And here's one more belief we might want to try out: *Things work out better for me when I keep my vibration as high as possible.* By that I mean that when I am as emotionally energized as I can be, the experiences I have are generally a lot better than when I am feeling down and have a low energy level. So, keeping my emotional state of being, my vibration, in a positive condition is of the utmost importance to me.

It is with this in mind that I then go on to decide that doing my best is good enough. Of course, I can choose to believe that it's not good enough, and then my energy falls and I become miserable. But by choosing to believe that my best is good enough, I allow my energy to stay high, I stop worrying about what I haven't done, and I keep my focus on enjoying the pleasures of my life.

Pleasure

Pleasure is very much a function of how we tell ourselves stories about our lives. If I say that the traumas that I endured as a child have scarred me and left me emotionally crippled as an adult, then I will likely be pleasure-impaired in my relationships and in my efforts to be successful. If, however, I say that the experiences of my childhood taught me to be self-reliant and powerful in spite of the very unpleasant nature of those experiences, then I am likely to feel good about myself and be able to enjoy the fruits of my efforts. Same childhood, different story.

Our pleasure is mostly a function of how we look at any given experience. In many ways we choose what's pleasurable to us and what's not. Having been a fine chef for many years, whenever I went out to restaurants I would expect good food and excellent service. Whenever I felt that things weren't up to par, I would become disgruntled and unhappy. When I finally realized that it was *I* who was making me unhappy, I decided that no matter how the food tasted or of what quality the service was, I was going to have a good time. From that point on, I always enjoyed my restaurant experiences.

Since we have the power to choose how we react to every one of our experiences, we want to select reactions that leave us feeling good. Of course, this means that we have to pay attention to how we're feeling in the first place. That's a handy habit to have at all times anyway.

We can react in lots of different ways to things we don't like. For many people disappointment is a given whenever what they expected doesn't quite happen as planned. Yet disappointment is only one of several choices we can make in reaction to what's in front of us. We can choose to find something else to focus on, or decide that whatever we expected isn't so important after all. Being mindful of the range of options we can choose from when we react to something gives us a freedom well beyond that of the habits we've grown into.

Let's not forget that we are free to enjoy as much of life as we want to. There is no limit to how much pleasure we can have in this lifetime. We could choose to regard this life as a veil of tears or that we are born into suffering and sin. But those are self-imposed limitations that we don't have to create. Lifting up our eyes and seeing the immense joy that is available to us any time we choose to look for it reminds us that we can live mostly in a state of great joy. And if we're not taking the time to enjoy the fruits of our labors thoroughly, why bother doing those labors in the first place?

These ideas bring us to the sacred art of savoring. Savoring is taking the *time* to enjoy something fully. It is not just stopping to smell the roses. It is breathing in the sweet fragrance and letting the pleasure of that experience seep into our full being. It is the awareness that we, as living animals, are a part of this Earth and that we, like all animals, are meant to enjoy life.

Savoring connects all parts of our being in one moment. Our minds are focused on the source of pleasure, our bodies are fully feeling that pleasure, and our Higher Mind is delighting in the harmony of that moment. Such a moment can occur at any time. It is not only grand experiences that are worthy of savoring. Every single moment has elements that are well worth savoring. And that is a crucial element of the happiness we all desire.

One of the kindest things we can do for ourselves is to stay focused on what's happening right now, right in front of us. This focus is being consciously present to ourselves. It involves nothing more than letting go of our thoughts about what did or did not happen in the past and ignoring our worries about what might happen in the future.

We've all been brought up with the idea that time goes from past to future, giving us a little space in between that we call "the present." This notion certainly seems to make sense. We have experiences that we remember or that other people tell us happened and we call them "the past." But, when we use our memories to bring up something that we have been holding onto from our past, that is a present time event. We are remembering something, but that "remembering" is happening right now. If we choose to, we can remember things differently by changing our focus a little or by changing our emotional reaction to the memory. And we do this in the present moment.

There are things which we imagine will happen, or might happen, and we call that "the future." The key word here is "imagine." The future is only in our imagination. We may quite sensibly say that we have seen patterns in our lives, and we can pretty accurately predict what will happen in the future in a lot of areas. We can say that if we boil milk, it will flow over the side of the pot. If we drive too fast, we will likely get a ticket or be in an accident. But at the moment when we are talking about the future, we are imagining what might happen. We are picturing what we think an experience will be although that experience has not yet arrived. This image is a present time event. It is only in the present that we imagine what the future might be. So essentially everything is happening in the present moment.

It is by consciously choosing to keep our focus on what's happening right now, at this moment, that we can savor the joys of our lives to the highest degree. Therefore, we can only be happy right now.

However, all pleasures come to an end. That's the nature of pleasure. It is an experience that is mainly dependent on novelty and contrast. As those things diminish, so does the experience of pleasure. There's no point in being unhappy that a given pleasure has gone, whether the source of that pleasure is not around anymore or we have tired of that experience.

Being sad or angry that a pleasurable situation is no more is a kind of grief. But it flies in the face of how life works. It's like being unhappy that youth is over or that a rollercoaster ride has come to an end. There's no point in not accepting the nature of things. However, by being thankful for what was and then shifting our focus to something enjoyable right now, or anticipating a future pleasure, we can be happy anytime we choose. Being at home in ourselves is being present to our inner experience as well as whatever is happening right now.

When we come home, we delight in the things and people we love. That is, we enjoy them, we appreciate them, we have fun with them; we find pleasure in them. Criticism, judgment, and shame all destroy the joy of the things and the people we love. So when we look at anything or anyone with any sense that they are not as perfect as we think they should be, we are letting go of our happiness and the pleasure of the moment. When we allow ourselves to enjoy whatever is happening to the greatest degree possible, without reservation, we come home to our own bliss.

The notion that there is something amiss with us is so prevalent that it could be called a national problem, or even a global problem.

It is an insidious toxic fog that permeates every aspect of our lives. But this shame, the idea that something is wrong with us, is continuously used to manipulate us. I don't want to suggest that this is some conspiracy. It is just how we have chosen to organize our society and the way we have accepted how things like advertising will motivate us to buy and how people with more power will "motivate" or manipulate others.

The idea that there is something deficient or improper about ourselves is a belief, a part of our operating system that we have accepted as real. We live with our beliefs so much it's like a fish in water. The fish wouldn't be able to tell you anything about water (even if it could talk) because the water is so pervasive that there is nothing to suggest that there could be anything different. And as long as we hold these limiting and harsh beliefs about ourselves, they affect everything we do. All of our endeavors at work, in love and romance, or simply our enjoyment of life are colored by these beliefs that there's something wrong with us.

We bruise our confidence and damage our ability to see our options clearly when we feed our shame. It affects how happy we allow ourselves to be. And it holds us back from enjoying the things we value the most. I define shame as *the choice* to disapprove of some aspect of ourselves. So when we choose to accept the notion that something is wrong with us, we shrink our vitality and our capacity to live.

Taking on any belief is a choice, whether it is made consciously or not. And it's a choice that can be changed at any time. We just need to recognize that it is a belief that we have adopted and have a willingness to take responsibility for it. That is, we don't have to say that we are responsible for putting a belief into our mind, but we do need to take responsibility for whether or not it stays there.

If we decide to change this belief for one that works better for us, then we are talking about self-love, which is the antidote for. It becomes a matter of rejecting any idea that says that we are less than other people, or some ideal, or perfection, or normal, or any other things or people we might compare ourselves to.

Just for the fun of it, suppose you were looking at a giant jigsaw puzzle of beautiful scenery. Allow yourself to see first the beautiful picture of the whole puzzle and then see all the pieces taken apart. See all the pieces laid out on the table randomly. Now pick up one piece. Let this piece represent you; it is the you-piece.

Look this piece over carefully and notice the brown or gray paper on the back side. Notice the meaningless colors on the shiny side of the piece. And pay attention to the protrusions and indents, the little peninsulas and bays of the piece. This piece is not like any other piece on the table. It is unique, distinct, and individual, just like you.

Now, in your mind's eye, let all of the other pieces come back together to reform the picture. It's still a beautiful picture, but it doesn't look quite right. It is missing a piece—the you-piece.

Before you put the you-piece back in the puzzle, notice that it would not fit if it were like any other piece. It just wouldn't work if you tried to replace it with another piece. The you-piece only works because of its uniqueness. So, go ahead and put the you-piece back in the puzzle and see how beautiful the whole thing is. And remember, it's only in its full beauty because of all the unique pieces there, including you.

While the world around us is apparently a real, objective one, the world we inhabit within ourselves is subjective. Each of us has our own version of this common realm. What we're talking about here is taking charge of our inner world so that we can enjoy it and feel fulfillment as much as possible. We do this by managing how we subjectively choose to respond to experiences and perceptions. We also have the ability to craft our experiences with our intentions and expectations.

Once we understand that it is our inner experience that affects the quality of our lives, we can then appreciate how much influence we have on our experiences. This is our true home. We are the ones who let the pleasure, the joy, and the love in or not. We are the ones who choose where we will find the things that gladden our hearts and excite us. We are the ones in charge of our happiness and the joy in our lives. No one else can give us these feelings unless we permit them to. No one can take them away unless we allow them to. We have the power to enjoy our lives by taking responsibility for what continues to live in our minds and hearts.

And when we have decided, for ourselves, that we choose happiness, then all of our decisions become based on whether or not these choices add to or detract from our happiness. This is what awaits us when we come home.

Meditation 1

Desire

From the moment I wake up in the morning, I am aware of desires. Maybe my first one is to go to the bathroom. Maybe the next one is to have some coffee or do some yoga or enjoy a morning walk. But once I fulfill one desire, at least one other desire takes its place. It seems like my day is just going from one desire to the next.

When I look around, everything I see has desires. The trees and all other plants desire sunlight and water. The birds and other animals desire food and shelter as well as freedom. Even water has desire; it runs downhill seeking places of peace and serenity.

Why do I want so much? Why do we all want so much? It seems that everything wants more than it has. It seems that there are things "out there" that we want to bring "in here" to help make us complete.

I see that desire is a basic law of nature. We have desires that motivate all of us to do things. We seek things that we think we need. And when I look at these desires, I can easily see that every one of these is motivated by a fundamental desire to feel better than we currently do.

This feeling good that I want, this pleasure, underlies everything I do. I may have conflicting desires because I want so many things. But each of them will help me feel good in its own way.

I can see that pleasure is the way I ultimately choose things. Somehow, I quickly calculate how much pleasure I expect, minus whatever pain might be involved, for each of my choices. I choose the one with the most overall pleasure, and that becomes the one I desire the most.

I know that all of my desires are okay. I may not understand all of my desires, but I know that there are no bad desires. I may not want to act on each of my desires, but that doesn't mean that there is anything wrong with these desires … or with me. I know that each of my desires is related to coming back into wholeness. And coming back into wholeness is the mother of all of my desires.

I know that I have secret desires and hidden yearnings for things I have not allowed myself to look at. These desires and yearnings have been buried for so long I'm not sure I can fully bring them into view. But I know they're there. And that's okay. When I feel safe enough, I'll look at them. There's nothing wrong with them. There's nothing wrong with me having those desires. There's nothing wrong with me at all.

I also know that the desires I hold on to and energize are the ones most likely to be realized. I like feeling my desires and anticipating the manifestation of those desires. Anticipation is such a sweet pleasure all by itself.

Some desires are like calls from the future, beckoning me to come in specific directions. I may not understand where these desires come from or where they are leading me, but I know that if I don't pay attention to them now, they will only get stronger. These desires aren't going to be denied. My choice with these kinds of desires is to either see where they will take me, or to fight them tooth and nail all along the way. I prefer not to fight them.

By remembering which of my many desires are the strongest, which of them I am most passionate about, I can focus my energies most effectively. Then small desires and urges won't distract me from the greater desires that guide my life. I love paying attention to my desires and getting down to the essence of them! When I ask myself, "What is it that I really want?" it brings me a clarity that makes life so much easier. When I choose what I genuinely want, the Universe seems to conspire to help me.

Living in such a big sea of desires, I'm glad I have a way to sort out which desires are the most important to me. I am happy with all my desires, even the strange ones. I am happy just being me.

When your soul awakens, you begin to truly inherit your life. You leave the kingdom of fake surfaces, repetitive talk and weary roles and slip deeper into the true adventure of who you are and who you are called to become. The greatest friend of the soul is the unknown. Yet we are afraid of the unknown because it lies outside our vision and our control. We avoid it or quell it by filtering it through our protective barriers of domestication and control.
The normal way never leads home.
John O'Donohue

Chapter 2

Calls to Come Home

There are many ways that we can receive signals to come home to ourselves. Some of them are subtle, but most of them are not. Home feels kind, comforting, nurturing. When we feel down, tired, dissatisfied, grumpy, unhappy, consistently anxious, or angry, then we are getting clear signals that we are not at home. We are not in alignment with our true selves at this point. And, what is most easily recognized, we aren't enjoying ourselves.

It's useful to remember here that the reality we are experiencing in the present moment is a function of what we are thinking, what we are feeling, and the multitude of beliefs we are holding. When we find that things aren't working the way we want them to, it's time to look at how we are creating this situation.

What we are experiencing in this moment must be accepted as it is. But we can make different choices tomorrow. We can decide that we want to change some things and have an experience that is unlike anything we have known before. There are lots of decisions we have previously made that still impact our lives. And other people may have influences on us as well. But most of the factors that make up what happens to us next are habits and patterns that we bring with us.

Nevertheless, there is another set of factors that is often overlooked as we make our way into tomorrow. These factors have the effect of being calls from the future, beckoning us to move in this direction or that. Sometimes it is these calls from the future that are the most active elements of our decision-making process, yet they seldom get credit for their impact.

These summoning impulses are often called desires, though sometimes we see them as attractions or fascinations. We generally have so many of these desires in a day that we don't stop to wonder where they all came from. Some of these desires we may be familiar with, like wanting to see old friends, eating a favorite food, or wanting to go on a specific vacation. Other desires seem to come out of the blue. Perhaps something awakens an unknown passion, or suddenly we crave an experience that we've never thought about before. Sometimes we become dissatisfied with our current experiences and our imagination hits on something novel that inspires us.

Whatever it is, something inside of us is urging us in some new direction. We have the choice to resist this calling or we can explore it. Creating the future that we desire is at the heart of this philosophy. Still, it's important to remember that we don't just create a beautiful future without some context. It is in listening to our desires that we pay attention to the lovely guidance and inspiration that is available at all times, whenever we ask for it. It is in this type of desire that things such as our life purpose, our personal cosmic explorations, or fate (if you like that idea) can be seen.

Rather than profoundly questioning what we think our calling is, it is much more useful to see what it is that we want to do. Some things that we desire to do, be, or have may not be practical in the present moment. Some things, like having a baby, becoming a doctor, or flying, require some preparation and planning. Some desires, if fulfilled, would bring us into conflict with the surrounding culture and make life severely tricky for us.

But all of these desires that seem to come from somewhere deep inside are calls to our wholeness, calls to come home to ourselves. They are voices of the future that are saying, "Look at me, if you want to be fully who you are. Come to me to be whole!"

There are no "bad" desires; there are just some desires that we probably don't want to fulfill in physical reality. Still, they all show us something about ourselves that's important. Often, people haven't permitted themselves to feel deeply into what they are most attracted to. There is too much stigma or taboo associated with our "deepest, darkest desires." So, I invite you to buck up your courage and permit yourself to explore those profound and powerful attractions, at least in your inner world!

What's your favorite feeling? Perhaps it's orgasm, being in love, or success come to mind. How about freedom, great speed, or simple tenderness? How about awe, profound emptiness, or giddiness? Really understanding which feelings you particularly like and which feelings are just okay may be more important than you think.

Very often we look at our possibilities from the perspective of what we think will benefit us the most. That's certainly very reasonable. However, being reasonable may well overlook the inner promptings we have that call us to new, un-thought of possibilities. We can only become aware of those inner promptings by feeling them. They reveal themselves in the unspoken language of subtle feelings and symbols. Knowing what to look for and being aware of their subtleties brings much greater clarity to those promptings.

One way of looking at feelings is that they are our experience of energy. Energy is movement, by definition. But it doesn't always move smoothly and evenly. In these human bodies of ours, we can block the free flow of energy with our muscles, and especially our fascia. We often do this to prevent the difficult feelings we may have from showing themselves in ways that we don't know how to deal with yet.

We tighten specific muscles to resist specific feelings. That's why it seems that memories are stored in the muscles. When we relax those muscles, the memory comes back. Another way of looking at this, and a way I find more useful, is that when we realize that certain muscles tighten, we can prepare ourselves to feel certain kinds of feelings when we relax them. Massage is wonderful and it helps us to relax in general, but trying to relax specific muscles without being prepared to deal with those particular feelings means that we will tighten those same muscles again until we're ready to fully feel those feelings. We do need to allow ourselves to feel those uncomfortable and sometimes scary feelings, but we don't need to hang out in those feelings. Generally, we just need to feel them fully and then they evaporate.

This is useful not only for optimizing how good we feel, but also for raising our vibration to levels that support our manifestations. The higher our vibration, the greater the energy we are putting out and the faster we manifest. Remember, the longing for one or more specific feelings dwells beneath every desire we have. When we tap into the feelings we want to have when we manifest what we want, it is much easier to bring this process to fruition.

By getting to know our feelings we become more comfortable with them, allow for more intensity in our feelings, and learn to relax enough to let them come and go through our system. I've often said that if you want to feel good, practice feeling good. Well, that's all well and good, but what kind of "good" do we want? If you put more attention on feeling good, you will become really expert at discerning what feeling feels better than other feelings. This is the work of a connoisseur.

Another important aspect of becoming a connoisseur of feelings is that the more sensitive you are to your feelings the faster you can process them and return to a flow state. This becomes a very effective spiritual path. Rather than being somewhat spiritually arrogant by saying that certain feeling states are inherently "better" than others, we simply say that if we keep consciously choosing to create the best feeling that appeals to us, in the long run we will naturally be drawn to the incredibly delicious feelings of the higher spiritual states. That process will happen in its own time and is a result of finding previously enjoyed pleasures not quite good enough.

The search for the increasingly better feelings cuts through the conceptual jungle that can easily entangle us on our journey. It is feelings, after all, that motivate us to seek the higher spiritual realms in the first place.

You don't get any cosmic points for being like someone else. The best you can hope for is to be happy, and you get that by being yourself. Understanding your authentic feelings and being okay with *all* of them is how you allow your happiness to arise in you. And by paying attention to what feelings you like the most and savoring those wonderful feelings you will vibrate at a level that brings forth more of those great feelings.

Science has us focus on cause and effect as though the present has predictably appeared, inexorably driven from the past. This idea looks at life mechanically, where each moment is the sum of all the moments before it. But this ignores the compelling ways that we are called to do or be something. From somewhere beyond any discernable past, new ideas and desires pull at us like an insistent little child. Their tug is irresistible. We can delay it or fight against it, but we can't hold it off forever. It's as though our future is summoning us to become who we were meant to be. Science doesn't have room for this, but our hearts do.

So, these calls from the future, or wherever, challenge us. They challenge us to become different. They never seem to invite us to stay in places of comfort or indolence. It's always some place that is at least a little uncomfortable, a little disorienting, but potentially much more pleasurable.

There was a garden in my dreams not long ago. It was the most vibrantly colorful garden imaginable. The reds and yellows were particularly striking, perhaps because the blues and greens were vivid background colors. It was intensity itself, clothed in color and shape. I reacted to it by being grateful that I had found it again and couldn't understand how I could have lost it. I had an explicit recognition that I both knew it well and longed to return and sit in it again.

This whole business of finding paradise and losing it, over and over, is quite compelling. One perspective is that we keep getting glimpses of it as we come closer, like the waterfall we are approaching on a hike. Another angle is that it calls to us when we most need the encouragement to go on. Like the Bali Hai of the musical *South Pacific*, it sings, "Come to me, come to me."

The Great Motivator of Life, Pleasure, whispers to us in dreams, as mine did. It appears as chance words from a friend or a book. Or it may reveal itself in works of art or nature. Sometimes soft words or images suddenly appear in our psyche. These subtle messages promise us something more, though, than just the experience of soon-to-be-attained pleasure. There is something in each message that says, "Follow me back to yourself." It's as though we're called by those pieces of ourselves that have been lost or neglected to bring them home.

Wholeness feels amazingly good. Each time we welcome some long-lost piece of ourselves home and accept it into our heart, we experience a rush of deep pleasure. It could be a sigh of relief at the letting go of some long-held resistance. It could be the surprise of seeing some unknown aspect of our personality. It could be an orgasm of epic proportions that has been waiting to come out for years.

When we look at these calls to wholeness, we might easily overlook the most mysterious of them, our attractions. Some of these attractions are easy to understand. A man of any age might easily be fascinated by a young woman. We might be attracted to a newborn animal, its "cuteness" drawing us in like powerful magic. We might be drawn to specific adventures or fields of knowledge. But some attractions defy easy understanding like pedophilia, kleptomania, and self-destructive behaviors.

We can assume that people who experience these kinds of attractions are somehow defective and we need to either "fix" them or marginalize them. Or we can assume that what these people are experiencing is a call to their own wholeness. As a society, we have plenty of experience of marginalizing those whose attractions are not understood and whose behavior based on these attractions is unacceptable to society. What if we said that those attractions are very healthy, but acting on them was not? Suppose we looked at how each of these people was attempting to resolve some conflict or inner problem within himself or herself. Yes, the actions based on these attractions or desires do violence to people and to the fabric of our agreed upon rules of behavior. We cannot condone nor allow those desires to be played out in action. However, the desires may be very helpful, not just for the individuals themselves, but for all of us.

What I'm suggesting is that attractions to things or activities beyond the bounds of our rules of society, whether we find them in others or ourselves, are not necessarily things to battle. When we fight against these attractions we are fighting ourselves. I suggest that we would profit by asking ourselves how these attractions serve us.

Could the pedophile be seeking acceptance of his own childhood sexuality? Could the kleptomaniac be exploring ways of coping with the perpetual frustration of unfulfilled desires? Could self-destructive behavior be an attempt to relieve emotional pain?

These possible explanations may not be accurate for any given person, but they give us an idea of how to move beyond "good" and "bad" in our understanding of these strange drives.

One of the difficulties with attempting to help those with antisocial attractions is that we may well find that the roots of these attractions lie in the disempowering attitudes and mores of our society. I do not blame culture for the actions of antisocial desires. The responsibility for our own actions belongs to each of us. However, our calls to wholeness take on more emphatic forms to overcome the resistances we create in our efforts to be "good" or "right." These calls get louder and louder. The emotions behind the dam build up, and when they spill over and the flooding begins, we complain about the flooding without taking any responsibility for the build-up in the first place.

Pleasure-negative approaches to life do not make sense, and they are destructive and hateful. To love is to accept who we are, as we are. Our desires and pleasures are at the core of our very being. I suggest that our calls to wholeness, no matter how wild or dangerous, are all efforts to bring us back into harmony with ourselves. And dreams of paradise and strange attractions are all ways in which something ahead of us is joyfully beckoning to us to come home.

We also need to be aware that we don't always interpret our desires accurately. I may want the love of a specific person and feel a devastating draw to that person, a pull that disrupts my entire life. However, it's much more likely that my desire is to be loved, and I have fixed my focus on that one person as though the love I want can only possibly come from him or her.

As was said before, the foundation of every single longing is a desire to feel better than we currently do. That means that if we look a little harder, we can find what it is that we want to *feel* in connection with each thing or activity that we want. Understanding the hidden desire then helps us to pinpoint our true desires more easily.

It's our deepest desires that drive us the most. Even if we can't identify them, they are a leading factor in how we craft our lives. If we can feel and get to know these hidden desires we can arrange things better to fulfill those desires. That requires us to delve deep into our psyches and feel around for what's there. That's plainly a daunting and perhaps scary task, but if we are going to come home to ourselves, we must take the path that goes through these woods.

Here's a short little warm-up exercise to help you identify which feelings you most desire. You may want to have someone read this to you, or you can record it for yourself. If you would like to hear me reading it, go to https://youtu.be/ZxcdoDWzKbg.

Take your time and feel each suggestion thoroughly. You might even want to do this more than once.

Miracle Max's Magical Jewelry Store

Picture yourself in a cobblestone alley in some ancient city on a bright sunny day. People come and go through this alley; there are lots of little shops here. The people are busily doing their daily shopping, some in a hurry and others meandering very slowly. But what is most interesting here is the curious little shop with the intriguing name—Miracle Max's Magical Jewelry Store.

Open the brightly colored door and step into Miracle Max's Magical Jewelry Store. Max himself is a kindly old man with a light step and a twinkle in his eye. He greets you warmly and invites you to come all the way in. The store itself is much bigger on the inside than it looks like it should be from the street. The walls and shelves are crowded with mysterious and magical things that you can wear. But the pride of his collection are a great many fascinating pieces of beautiful jewelry, like talismans, rings, necklaces, and crowns, which can make you feel any way you like. Each piece in this collection evokes a particular feeling. Miracle Max invites you to try on different items of jewelry to see how you resonate with that feeling. Take your time; there's no rush here.

So try on a golden crown of power and influence and see how that feels. Now try on a brightly polished ring of insight, clairvoyance, and wisdom. Now try on a diamond brooch of great wealth. Try on a wooden earing of great humility. Try on little silver wings of freedom. Try on a simple bracelet of peace and comfort. Try on a colorful badge of great success and accomplishment.

And now try on an elegant necklace of self-esteem and self-love, and see how that feels. Try on a splendid pendant of warm personal connections. Try on a bright pin of commitment and reliability. Try on a little chain of reverence and awe. Try on a bold choker of sexiness and desirability. Try on a shiny badge of nobility and virtue. Try on a sparkly hoop of great passion.

Try on anything else there that appeals to you.

If you could buy only one thing from Miracle Max, what would it be?

Besides looking at the future as merely the inevitable result of things that have occurred in the past, modified by whatever choices we are making in the present moment, another useful way to look is to see ourselves standing on the precipice of the future. Before us lies a great abundance of possibilities to choose from for our next step. At any one moment there may be a limited number of probabilities.

But each selection opens an array of other choices that then go on to give us unlimited possibilities.

Depending on what we are feeling and in what state of vibration we are operating, we will use the natural process of deciding which option seems to offer us the highest overall pleasure and go for that one. However, our grander desires significantly influence that process. What are the things and feelings that draw us forward on the deeper levels of our being? If we haven't taken the time to explore these desires their impact on us will be minimal. We will then have to make choices that don't approach our deepest needs until we get to the point of sufficient dissatisfaction where we can't help but look for what's missing. That dissatisfaction is a gift at whatever stage it appears, and the sooner we accept it, the quicker we can come home.

We all experience dissatisfaction many times a day. We taste our food and adjust the amount of salt and pepper because we are very mildly dissatisfied with the concentrations as presented to us. We roll over in bed because we no longer thoroughly enjoy our previous position. We change the channel on our television sets because we have become dissatisfied with the current station. These are petty dissatisfactions, but the ones surrounding our jobs, our relationships, or our living space are very similar, only larger. Discontents of any size lead to desires. And it is what we do at this point that determines whether we utilize our dissatisfaction or let it go to waste.

There are many ways of dealing with dissatisfaction. Ones that are easy to change, like your position in bed, get changed, and that's the end of it. But there are lots of moments of dissatisfaction that challenge us to make serious changes. One of the most classic responses to dissatisfaction is complaining, especially complaining without doing anything further. I'm sure we all know people who specialize in complaining, and who never really have an answer to the question, "Well, why don't you do something about it?"

Related to the complaining tactic is the one of enduring and resignation. One usually assumes that anything they might do wouldn't do any good anyway. Since the motivation to do anything is to feel better than one is feeling in the moment, the person is in effect saying, "If I endure this, it is better than all the pain and wasted effort of trying to make things different." There may also be an element of preferring the numbness engendered in enduring to the possibility of some unknown pain.

Some people feel better when situations of misery or unhappiness validate their rules of reality. If their view is that "The world is against me," and events and circumstances keep occurring that support that view, then these people at least have the satisfaction of knowing that they were right. Undoubtedly there are a great many other responses to dissatisfaction that the talented minds of mankind have developed. But the one that interests me the most is that of appreciating dissatisfaction for what it can teach us and motivate us to do.

For one thing, dissatisfaction puts us in touch with our inner guidance system, the one that shows us when we are in alignment (or out of alignment) with the deepest parts of ourselves. When we are feeling dissatisfied, we know that our higher being is urging us towards finding something else that will suit us, in our totality, better. If, for instance, we like drinking a lot of alcohol because we enjoy the effects of that inebriation, at some point the pleasure of that inebriation will diminish to the point where there is dissatisfaction with that inebriation. This awareness occurs best when there is little interference by ideas of what should or should not be done. It is a process of self-awareness and needs its own space to develop in. Relationships, jobs, living situations, and appearance can all go through this process.

Dissatisfaction, when we take the time to look it over carefully, shows us what works for us, and what doesn't. We ask ourselves, "Does this work for me?" It is dissatisfaction that alerts us to the likelihood that whatever this is, it doesn't cut it. By trying to conform to standards and ideas of how things "should be" we short-circuit our guidance system. We overrule or simply ignore the signs of dissatisfaction in the name of doing something "right." The more we do this, the further we get away from who we truly are. We lose sight of our personal wisdom and rely on the opinions of others to tell us what to think and how to feel.

Dissatisfaction can empower us. By acknowledging that we don't have to endure, that complaining may get us only sympathy or miserable company, and that validation of one's ideas about reality is a paltry pleasure, we move into a position to change things dramatically.

Dissatisfaction is the first step in reclaiming our core being. It is the statement that "This isn't good enough for me!" When we can say that, we are ready to look around for what might be good enough. We start to become connoisseurs of life, seeking out the things that excite us, that bring us joy, that spark delight, and magically entrance us. Our choices, the options that our mind presents us with, become based on what would please us the most, not on what will relieve our fears the most.

It all begins when we honor our dissatisfaction and let it motivate us to live and feel even better than ever before!

Passions

Perhaps the most obvious of the calls to come home are our passions. These are those intense feelings that seem to be more than just simple desires; they are like powerful forces that rise like a volcanic eruption to fill our minds with an unruly imperative. These are not the "passions" of anger and hate, but rather the true passions of recognition of an inner calling from our very being.

Passions have a nasty reputation in some circles. They get accused of taking people into dangerous and destructive places from which misery is inevitably the only outcome. Passions are often likened to fire; they are intense and can be dangerous if the fire isn't kept contained. But, if the fire is controlled, it can do wondrous things. In the same way, if passions are out of control, there is a huge potential for disaster. However, if the person uses his or her passions with wisdom and flexibility, then powerful and beautiful things flow naturally. Passions get out of control when a person loses perspective, when the passion is the only consideration, and when he or she overlooks all their other needs and desires. Held in balance and context, passions give us the energy to fuel our creativity.

When we do something that we are passionate about, it is the feeling that we have while we are doing it that is what is so great. Getting something done is nice, but the fabulous aspect of this is the feeling of excitement that we have while doing it.

Think of something that excites you. If nothing else comes to mind, allow yourself to think of someone or something sexual or erotic that excites you. While holding on to the image or thought, pay attention to the feeling. Generating this feeling is what will energize your engine of creation. Think of some of the things that excite you that you would like to do in your life. Now find the one that is the biggest, most exciting one and hold on to it. It is this excitement that energizes our lives and makes them worth living.

Sometimes we embody these calls from within in ideas of what the best life could be or should look like. The world is full of principles and divine instructions. A simple look at the teachings found in the world's religions shows a profound array of do's and don'ts. However, these directives often drown out our inner promptings, and then we overlook the wealth of information and suggestions coming from our core being. As wise as the teachings of others might be, it is only in listening to our own wisdom that we can find our way home. We relieve the cacophony of instructions telling us how we should live by making our voice the most important one.

Developing our inner dialogue is more than just listening; it is also asking for the information we want. It's beneficial to decide what it is we'd like to know and then ask directly for that. We invite our inner voice to say things, in whatever fashion that works at the moment, that are useful and that help us to grow and evolve.

By using the calls of desire and dissatisfaction, we go along a path that shows us new panoramas of consciousness and joy. Each time we let go of something that is no longer "good enough," we open ourselves to things that can be even better. Each time we release what we were yesterday, we create a new perception of ourselves that is closer to our natural being.

Meditation 2
Savoring Myself

I create myself in different ways each day. Today I have been a little different than I was yesterday. And today I have tried to do things even better than before. I found out a little more about myself today. And I enjoyed something new. I like that, and I like spending a few moments just enjoying being me.

Sometimes it amazes me when I think that I am creating my own reality in this moment. I am not conscious of most of the things going on inside me, but I know that all these beliefs and ideas and imaginings are showing up in my waking life.

I look to see how I am creating myself at this moment. I craft each moment with my ideas, my feelings, my desires, and my overall attitude. It is a creation that expresses my soul. I savor the wondrous creative act of being me today.

I am aware of my unique perspectives and perceptions. These are my opinions and beliefs, the things that tickle my funny bone, my sense of style, what a great adventure looks like to me, and the people who energize me the most. All of these perspectives and perceptions go into making me who I am today, and I enjoy each of them.

I think about the colors that perk me up, the activities that give me the most satisfaction, the music I like, and my comfort foods. I let these pleasures fill me up, and I recognize that these are the things that make me who I am.

I savor the things that I have already created or have helped to create in my life. I have put considerable effort into accomplishing things. I have achieved many things in my life, some I thought were big and some I thought were small. But they were all some kind of success. I savor all the big and little triumphs of my life.

Over the years I have created many living environments that have suited me. Perhaps there are things I'd like to do to improve the living situation that I now experience, but there is a great deal about it that I like. I savor how much I love this environment and how good I feel when I am in it.

I take time to savor the relationships that I have enjoyed, the connections I have built, and all the fun times with people that I have helped to create. As I think about these things, I feel the joy of being connected to them. These connections have been vital to me, and I cherish the memories of all of them.

I think about those things now that I want to create. I consider the different aspects of my living environment that I would like to change or add. I think about artistic expressions, big and small, that I would like to put my energies into. I think about the wonderful relationships with people, animals, or the earth that I would like to create.

Each of these acts of creation is an expression of me. So, I savor myself as I prepare to go forth to do those things that I want to accomplish. I savor myself as I venture out to create new things in my life. I savor myself as I expand my capacity for love and joy. I savor myself as I become more fully who I am as a human *being.*

I am grateful for this gift of life. I am alive, and I savor this amazing experience. It is a magnificent gift!

I am an expression of All-That-Is, and I have the power to enjoy it thoroughly.

It's Time to Come Home

We need to see, and agree that what we seek already lives within us, and we within it. Now we know our one great task: watch for whatever promises us freedom, and then quietly, consciously refuse to see ourselves through the eyes of what we know is incomplete. Then we live wholeness itself, instead of spending our lives looking for it.
Guy Finley

Chapter 3

Outfitting Ourselves for Our Trek Home

Once we have decided to make the effort to come home to ourselves, we have begun an extraordinary adventure. There will be dangers, surprises, awe-inspiring insights, never-imagined opportunities, and an ever-increasing joy that will amaze us with its beauty and glory.

However, like any real adventure, there are things that we need to outfit ourselves with to make this journey as comfortable as possible. We can't foresee everything; we probably don't even want to. But we want to make ourselves ready for the surprises as best we can. There are also several valuable tools for dealing with the fog, the impassable rivers, and the jungles ahead of us. We don't need to master these tools entirely before we embark. But, not understanding these skills at least partially is what has allowed us to get off track.

Focus

Probably the most essential tool that needs as much skill as we can muster is that of being able to focus. Being able to control what we are focusing on is vital to discerning our way through the myriad distractions that are always present. We use the tool of focus to decide which thoughts and which feelings we will allow to remain in our field of vision. We move our focus from one thing to another or keep that focus on one thing.

What we focus on tends to enlarge and get more energized. For instance, when we permit the focus of our thoughts to dwell on what might happen to us and we go into the depths of our fears, we lose any sense of perspective and power. We become entirely absorbed in our victimhood. Our fears become so "real," and we become so "helpless" that we become paralyzed. On the other hand, when we put our attention on the things we enjoy and love, we feel a lovely sense of peace and tranquility that increases the longer we hold our focus there.

I have a friend who has become something of a master at taking something that *might* be of concern and turning it into the most terrible danger imaginable. She gets so worked up that she becomes a wreck trying to figure out how she will cope with the dangers that she has just imagined. It's more than a toxic obsession with "what if?" It's channeling all her energy into the places where she feels awful, not only about the world, but even more detrimentally, about herself. And, as far as I can tell, feeling bad about oneself is about the worst experience we can have.

The power of focus is very much like the reins on a horse at our command. A horse is a very powerful animal, and its importance in the history of mankind can't be overstated. But it isn't the only hard-working animal out there, nor is it even the most powerful one. It is useful to us both because it is powerful and because it can be controlled. In the same way, we use our focus to guide and direct our attention. We need to have some control over what our mind is doing and what we are consciously or unconsciously creating for ourselves.

So, just like controlling a horse, we need a way to regulate what we are aware of and what we are ignoring. With a horse, that control is conveyed through the reins from the rider to the horse.

When we let go of the reins and find that we are not in charge of our focus, we set ourselves up to be manipulated by events, other people, and most worrisomely, our own imagination. Holding onto our centeredness is the key to keeping our focus where we want it. But, what do we do when our attention and imagination (or our horse) are running away with us? Just as with the horse, the first thing to do is to grab the reins and pull back. Everything needs to come to a halt before anything else happens.

Calming down is the operative task here. In fact, saying the word "calm" over and over can help all by itself. Like many mantras that end with an "mmm" sound, the word "calm" allows the very soothing "mmm" sound to vibrate through the skull and relax the body.

Once the uncontrolled racing through "dangers" is brought to a halt, we can turn our focus, the inner equivalent of the reins, to things that will serve to help in whatever situation we find ourselves.

There are three steps we can use to take charge of our reins and our focus. The first is to recognize that we are in charge of what we focus on—or at least, we can be. For many of us, our focus is powerfully influenced by the world around us, and especially by the media. Television commands our attention and changes our focus at will. Our friends and loved ones can demand our attention as well, and we have no apparent choice of whether to focus on them or not. But we do, in fact, have a choice. We can choose to focus on something else instead.

The second step is to become aware of how we feel about what we are currently focused on. What are we feeling, and how do we feel about feeling that way? In other words, does this work for us? Are we focusing on things that make us feel good and powerful or not? Without this understanding we have no reference point. We can't make an informed choice about whether or not to change our focus. But when we can see that what we are focusing on is making us miserable, then we have the motivation to shift that focus to something that is more pleasant for us.

We have to have a certain amount of self-confidence to be able to say that what the media wants us to worry about probably isn't worth any worry at all. This self-confidence comes from deciding to be the authority in our lives, and that's a very useful decision. It's not a one-time decision; we need to keep making it as new challenges to our personal authority arise. But once we start, it becomes a delightful and useful habit.

The third step is to choose how we want to feel and then what we will focus on that will give us that feeling. If I am feeling annoyed at how I'm being treated in a car repair shop, for example, I can decide to stay annoyed and savor the feeling of annoyance. Or I can conclude that annoyance is overrated and that I want to feel loving instead. So I can simply think of the people I care about in this world. Perhaps I might think about the people I will get to help in the near future, or even think of all the things that have happened to me lately that have been helpful to my health and well-being. All that has happened is a deliberate change of focus. It's as simple as that.

We don't have to avoid problems that need our attention. A clear awareness of what needs to be done and a commitment to do it will suffice for now. We don't need to avoid painful feelings that arise. Merely feeling them and shifting our focus as they subside will do. We are choosing what we focus on as best we can with an awareness that our feelings arise from what we put our attention on. And when we have mastered to some degree the skill of focus, we can choose to be happy whenever we want. So I like to say that it pays to pay attention to what we're paying attention to.

When we set out for a serious adventure into unknown territory, we'd never go without a good compass and the best map we can find. But we'd also want to pay close attention to our hiking shoes. The things we use in every moment can be overlooked, and yet are extraordinarily important. Just like hiking shoes, our thoughts need to fit us well, and we need to make sure that we are using them correctly. We are embarking on this adventure to feel good. If we start out with shoes, or thoughts, that don't make us feel good, we're in for some serious trouble.

The connection between thoughts and feelings is so apparent that it's hard to believe that we might have missed it all along. We think of someone we care deeply about, and we start to feel good. We think about something we don't want to do, and we begin feeling sour and down. This is such a simple mechanism that to feel good most of the time is merely to have thoughts that make us feel good intentionally. Certainly, in the course of living life there will be plenty of times when we need to pay attention to things that don't make us feel good. But when that's been taken care of to whatever extent is possible in that moment, we want to choose to return our focus to pleasurable thoughts.

Relaxation

In many senses, the entirety of the spiritual path of coming home and the key to inner exploration is about relaxation. We tense up when we are out of alignment with our Higher Self/Spirit/God/the Universe, and we relax when we come back into alignment. This is our natural guidance system, and it works all the time. The key to relaxation is to enjoy being who we are without criticism, judgment, or doubt. That's also called self-love.

The most essential relaxation is *relaxing into intensity*. All the great feelings in this world—love, joy, peace, harmony, happiness, to name just a few—are intense. These beautiful experiences can easily overwhelm us, and it may take some time to get used to the strength of these feelings. But as we go along our homeward path, we will have a great many feelings to process. Some of these feelings may be fears that we have stifled for years. Others may be emotional pains from rejection or abandonment. Still others may be the disappointment of dreams that meant a great deal to us at one point but had to be abandoned.

The key to working through all of the strong feelings is to relax into them long enough for them to be fully felt. Once we have experienced the feeling thoroughly, it will magically disappear. While we may have a fear that this vast emotion might hang around forever, they never do once the energy behind them is unblocked.

There are many potent techniques for relaxing into the deeper feelings we have and working with the felt sense of the contours of our inner world. Many of these are therapeutic in nature and may be useful for dealing with "issues." Particularly be aware of the inner tensions that come with merely thinking the thoughts we all have. We can choose our thoughts, and in so doing we choose how we are feeling, for the most part. There are no rules about what thoughts we should or should not have, so why not choose the ones that help us feel better about ourselves?

When we find that we have increased our internal tension due to specific thoughts or ways of thinking, we can modify our overall vibration or energetic level of being by relaxing. We can relax whether we are merely sitting alone, in contemplation, or in meditation. There is no need to be on a state of high alert all the time; that doesn't serve us. An awareness of any stress or tension lets us consciously do something about it.

This kind of awareness is a skill that needs to be developed over time. The more we learn to simply relax in almost all situations, the more we take back our power. We'll work with this later in this book. But for now, it is enough just to recognize the importance of this simple act. Relax!

Most physical discomforts, and that includes a great many aches, pains, and hurts, can be the result of stress related to specific thoughts. "He gives me a pain in the neck!" "Every time I see her, I get a stomach ache." "I get a headache whenever I think about what I need to do." These are physical reactions to thoughts with high emotional content. One handy way of dealing with them is to recognize that each of these discomforts has a specific set of muscles that have tightened to the point of pain. By thinking the particular thought, noticing which muscles have tightened up, and intentionally relaxing those muscles in the area of tension, we can retrain our body to react to that particular thought in a different, and more comfortable, way. This is a great way to develop our awareness of the connection between our thoughts and feelings.

Most empowered spiritual philosophies place great emphasis on learning this retraining technique. And, when you get deeply enough into relaxation, it even becomes a conscious effort to tighten up enough to think with words. This space below the level of verbal thought is where we can do some of our most exciting explorations.

Compassion

We usually think of compassion in terms of feeling a sense of other people's pain and suffering and a concurrent feeling of wanting to do something to alleviate that suffering. Compassion is a highly esteemed feeling in most religions, especially Buddhism. Without compassion we move through life without the connections to others that make life worthwhile.

But what is compassion, really? Yes, it's a feeling. But it's also a focus, a focus on what we imagine is another person's experience. We can never really know what another person is undergoing, but we can certainly resonate with what we can perceive with our senses, both our inner senses and our outer ones. Compassion is an acknowledgment that we are involved in the lives of all other living beings on Earth. For some people that acknowledgment focuses on the humans in their immediate circle. For others, the focus extends out to all humans or even all things everywhere. But however it is experienced, it is an awareness of something within us. As an inner event, we can become aware of the lack of set boundaries between our deeper being and other beings everywhere. We can feel an impression or sense of the higher realities of which we're a part. And it feels amazingly delightful!

So, what does compassion *for ourselves* mean? Compassion happens when we view the world, others, or anything from a place apart from our regular operating pattern, with our hearts open. We witness, with both our intellect and our emotions, what is happening from a slightly detached perspective that lets us see it from a wider angle. When we take such a view of ourselves, we can be aware of both our experience and how we feel about that experience.

Here's a little exercise around being compassionate toward yourself. Think of something in your life that hurts, either physically or emotionally. Just let your attention rest on the pain. At this point, don't try to ease the pain or do any healing. Just pay attention to how you feel about having this pain. Obviously, you don't like it. But what else do you feel? See if you can be aware of the pain in a broader context, as in how much pain is this compared to other pains you've had? How does this pain compare to the pain you've seen in others? What can you learn from this pain? In the context of your life, on a scale of 1 to 10, how significant is this pain? And, most importantly, what does this pain teach you? What lessons can be gleaned from this experience? Once you've harvested whatever you might learn from this pain, both about you and about others in pain, do what you need to do in order to lessen or remove the pain. Let the pain be your teacher for a short while before asking or telling it to leave.

Imagination

Imagination is the fourth tool that we want to pack in our kit. This is so important, yet so pervasive, that it's easy to overlook it. We use imagination in *everything* we do. We envision each action we intend taking just before we begin. We imagine the possibilities of each choice to calculate the relative pleasure of each option. We direct our energies with our imagination to make things happen. There is nothing we do that doesn't involve our imagination.

Neuroscience has shown that the same parts of the brain light up when we are imagining experiencing something as they do when we are actually experiencing that something with our physical senses. Just by pre-imagining an experience, you will become very comfortable with it even before it shows up for you.

The inner world, at least for humans, seems to work primarily in symbols and metaphors. We create metaphors for our experiences all the time. In exploring ourselves, we select the metaphor we'd like to work in and then ask for our experience to be in terms of this metaphor.

If, for example, I want to tackle some complex project, I might want it think of it in military terms. I decide on the objective, muster my troops, deploy my energies, and proceed to knock down all the obstacles in my way. I would invite the people and organizations that would be helpful to be allies in my campaign and to participate in their own ways.

Or I might want to think in terms of farming, where I would prepare my soil carefully, plant my seeds in deliberate rows, water and fertilize my sprouting crop, and mindfully remove the weeds as they appear. I could then ask the elements of nature to work with me to maintain the right conditions for me to reach a bountiful harvest.

Or I might want to use a cooking metaphor. I would select the needed ingredients and prepare them for the dish. I would then cook each ingredient in a way that would optimize its texture and flavor. And then I would assemble everything for the final presentation. My fellow diners would play their critical part: eating it. There is no point to cooking a wonderful dish if there is no one to enjoy it.

All of these metaphors give us a way to frame the project in order to think it through clearly. The active imagination, where we consciously create the scene, gives way to the passive imagination, where the players in the scene show us what they can do. By giving ourselves a framework within our imagination, we make it possible to learn things and accomplish things in a non-physical way. Tibetan Buddhists, who are particularly good at this, use imagination frequently to create useful realities for themselves.

In coming home to ourselves, it's beneficial to think of the peace, love, harmony, or whatever else we want to enjoy at the deepest levels of our being. Now imagine that you are experiencing some especially delightful version of home. Be aware of all your senses in this experience. Pay attention to the *pleasure* of this experience you have desired. Live this experience for as long as you can hold your focus on it. This is a powerful and effective use of the tool of imagination.

Trust Yourself

The fifth item that we don't want to overlook when we're packing is self-confidence. Now, self-confidence is a characteristic of having come home to ourselves. It's not fair to say that you need to already be at home in order to get home. But there are significant ways that we can simulate that confidence to make it seem more real. This is a matter of learning to choose to trust.

> *Just trust yourself, then you will know how to live.*
> Johann Wolfgang von Goethe

Trust isn't just a concept we use to refer to our willingness to let something happen without our interference. It is a way we hold our bodies in a relatively relaxed fashion. It's a very different body sensation from doubt. There is tension with doubt that's absent in trust. And that difference in body-feel is reflected in the vibration we send out into the world.

When we want to manifest something, anything from a new car to just a pleasant day, our success or failure is dependent on the vibration we hold when we are focused on our desire. In general, the higher we keep our vibration, the more pleasurable our experience will be. By keeping our vibration high, I mean intentionally feeling as good as we can.

We all have the means to adjust how we feel. As noted, what we focus on, which is always our choice, is generally what determines how we feel. If I focus on the beauty around me, I will feel good. If I focus on the stupidity of politicians, then I'm likely to feel angry or sad. I can then change my feeling-state by shifting my focus. However, the one thing that challenges everyone is doubt.

In my experience, when doubt arises it seems to commandeer my mind. It seems to take over my will to focus on what I choose. My body can feel tight, and my breath is contracted. Doubt is a very visceral, body-oriented phenomenon. If I continue to let it reign over me, my vibration deteriorates dramatically and nothing seems to go right.

It's at this point that I need to wrest control of my vibration back from doubt. Sometimes, I can just tell doubt to go away. And sometimes it responds to that command. Sometimes I can reason with it and calm it down by mentally demonstrating that the doubts and fears are not reasonable and that there's nothing to be concerned about. However, there are also plenty of times when nothing mental or logical seems to help overcome my fear. It takes something more.

The conflict is happening in my body, and I think the solution needs to be a body-based one. My body is concerned for its well-being, but I'm going to have to make a choice about how I'm going to take care of it. Staying in the vibration of doubt is both dangerous and unhealthy. So, I'm going to have to change my vibration, and do so quickly.

So I choose to hold a vibration of trust. I do that by willing myself to focus on expecting good things to happen. I can expect anything I want to, and if I am not expecting other people to do anything in particular, my expectations usually work out.

But that's not why I hold the vibration of trust. I do so because I create or manifest the things I want much more smoothly when my vibration is high. There may be no logical reason to choose to trust, but when I do, I get better results. My body calms down, my thinking processes work better, I am more open to inspiration and insight, I am not emotionally paralyzed, and people around me respond to me better.

This is why faith works so well for many people. It's not really about believing in something believable (although believability helps). It's about how a person can go through life without being crippled by cynicism or worry.

I've had times when things looked so bleak that I could hardly get out of bed in the morning. I couldn't see any possibility for a successful solution to my problems. In those times I often just pushed on forward for lack of any other option. But the times when I blindly said that I would trust the Universe to make things right, somehow It always did.

It's that proverbial *leap of faith* that bypasses logic and opens the door to good things happening. So I find that holding that vibration of trust when I don't see my way clearly is what gives room for the little miracles that come.

The choice to trust that things are working out perfectly is what allows things to work out perfectly.

A Willingness to Ask for Help

You don't have to do this process alone. Not only are there many people around you who can guide you in this practice, but you can also ask questions of the unseen world and get useful answers. This is the sixth major tool to take along with you.

It doesn't matter who or what you ask for assistance from, the very act of asking for help does several things. It relieves you of some of the burden of feeling that you have to do it all yourself. It lets you trust that most of the other details are being taken care of as you focus on your intention. And you tap into the intuitive parts of yourself and open yourself up to guidance.

This is why we use deities, saints, angels, ancestors, power animals, and spirit guides. They, and many others, are all ways of tapping into supporting wisdom that we feel comfortable with. But just asking for help without any kind of form or symbol in mind works just as well.

The answers may come in a wide variety of ways, but most often the asker just has an inner knowing, a sense of the answer, in their awareness. Since this existence is based on free will, questions that start with, "Should I do …" won't go far. If life were a matter of just getting it right, it would be exceedingly boring. A more useful view is to think of life as an adventure or an exploration. We don't put the emphasis on doing what we're supposed to do. Instead, we focus on what we can learn and how we can grow.

So questions along the lines of "Would you recommend I try…?" or "Is this path a useful one for me?" work much better. Since we are working in a free will arena, we are rarely going to be told what to do by anything we want to listen to. But fear has no compunction about telling us what to do or giving us explicit instructions. True wisdom never tells us what to do, it only offers us useful options. This is an easy way to distinguish between wisdom and fear.

Trust the Adventure

The seventh and last of the essential tools that you want to bring with you is a trust in the adventure of life. Again, this is a choice to trust. It doesn't mean that everything will work or happen the way you want it to. It means that you trust that whatever is happening right now is useful to you in the greater arena of your life. Let's not forget that the most substantial part of your existence is not physical. You have a great many things going on that, while they may be ignored, affect your well-being and growth tremendously. If you allow yourself the belief that your life is working out well, no matter what, the things going on in your life will be a lot easier to handle.

Your primary power in life is in your ability to choose. You can choose to just go with the flow, like a log floating down a raging river. Or you can choose to be like a whitewater rafter and use your paddles to direct your raft in ways that keep you from hitting rocks, getting caught in whirlpools, or being shunted off into some useless eddy.

In the same way, you can choose what it is that you'd like right now and then choose to trust that it will appear in your life at the right time. Remember that trust is a choice you can make, and you can choose to trust that you will be okay with whatever happens next.

There are no guarantees, but things just seem to work out better when you make the choice to trust Spirit. After you have done your preparation work it is time to stop *trying* and shift into *allowing*. You've launched your intentions, raised your personal vibrations, and opened your heart. You've done the footwork, and the last piece is to trust that some higher part of your awareness got the purchase order and is preparing whatever is best for your higher good and the good of all.

Moving into the unknown creates a spaciousness for us; the unknown is where mystery and possibilities exist. And that's where we're most alive.

Here's a simple little exercise to make this point clear. Picture yourself standing on a high cliff. The air is cool, and the sun is bright. You can see clouds ahead of you at the same height that you are. There are people around you looking over the cliff, as well. One by one, they jump off the cliff and fall until they learn that they can fly. Each one who has jumped off has figured out how to fly.

Now it's your turn. You probably don't know how to fly, but the other people didn't either. So lean forward until you start to fall. Trust that you will be okay. Let yourself fall and fall until you decide to start flying. You may not actually understand what you're doing, but just the will to fly will do the trick. Just choose to fly and you will. So fly!

Fly out away from the cliff. Fly towards the sun and the clouds. Fly around others who are flying, or fly around some birds. Enjoy the feeling of freedom as you fly. Explore the fun of flying for a while.

Meditation 3
Self-Love

Quietly, I let my tensions drain away. As my breath gets softer, I feel my feet relax. My calves relax, and so do my thighs. My hips relax, and my buttocks do, too. My back relaxes all the way up my spine. My belly relaxes, and so does my chest. My hands and fingers relax. My arms and shoulders relax. My neck relaxes, and so does my throat. My tongue relaxes as well as my face. My eyes relax, and my ears do too. My scalp relaxes, and all the tensions of the day drain away.

I'm thankful for this body of mine. It's such a miracle of creation. I'm grateful that it works as well as it does. I'm thankful for all the pleasures I experience with my body, both the big, grand pleasures and all the beautiful little pleasures, too.

I'm grateful for all the love in my life, all the people I get to love and who love me, all the animals I get to love, all the plants and other aspects of nature I get to enjoy, and all the beauty that I encounter every day.

I let go of all the things that may have upset me today. I choose to be happy and let go of all those things that don't contribute to my happiness. I love being happy and do what I need to do, to stay happy most of the time.

I do the best that I can each and every day. And that's enough. I don't need to do or be better than my best. I am a human being, and I can only do my very best. I let the Universe take care of all the rest. I am enough.

I am not just like anyone else; I am unique. My body is like others, but no one else's is just like mine. My thoughts are mine alone and so are my feelings. Even my spirit is a little different from all the others.

It's good that I am unique so that I can contribute to the world in my own special way. I am an essential piece of the puzzle of life. No one else fills that role the way I do. My voice is an important one in the choir of life.

I am the authority in my life. Other people may advise me and make valuable suggestions, but I am the one who decides how I will craft my life. I am the one who takes responsibility for the decisions I make. I am the one who decides what is right and what is wrong for me. I am the sovereign of my life.

I am free to be who I am. I am free to be me. I am free to express the essence of my being. I may decide not to share everything with everyone. But I am free to be the person that I am entirely. There is nothing wrong with me. I am just fine the way I am.

I love the little things that make me who I am. I love my favorite foods, the clothes I choose to wear, and the things I find witty. I love the things I create, like my bedroom, my appearance, and my relationships.

I love how I love other people. I enjoy helping others. I love showing other people that I care. I love helping others when I can.

I love taking good care of myself. I love nurturing my body and making sure that it stays as healthy as possible. I love nurturing my mind and giving it the challenges and exercise it needs. I love to nurture my heart, and I choose to love whenever I can.

I love, and that love expands every day in all directions.

And the true order of going is to use the beauties of Earth as steps along which one mounts upwards for the sake of that other Beauty.
Plato

Chapter 4

We Come Home to Feel Good

When we look at our lives from the perspective of pleasure, we get to the root of our decision-making process. All our decisions are based on the desire to feel better than we currently do. Then we very often create rationales for explaining the reasonableness of the decision that we just made, though very likely it was solely based on feeling good.

Pleasure is more about what we decide to enjoy than anything inherently pleasurable. It is as much about our imagination as it is about feelings and experience. This is the key to truly enjoying life: deciding to appreciate what we have rather than looking for more and more things that we hope will give us pleasure.

Whatever we choose to guide our lives, it is something that makes us feel good. When we recognize that we are always looking for ways to increase our positive feelings, the degree of agreeable feelings versus unpleasant feelings becomes our guidepost. By being aware of how we feel and our relative pleasure at any given moment, we have an inner compass to steer by. When we link to our inner guidance at our core, we feel good. When we are fighting our inner selves, we feel bad. All of our ideas about what is good and bad, healthy or unhealthy, and right or wrong come down to how they make us feel.

This sounds simple enough and easy to do. So why aren't we all extraordinarily happy?

The simple answer is that we don't know how to do it. Oh sure, we know when something feels good and when something is painful. But that begs the question, how can I make my life less painful?

The more complicated answer is that we have been taught a great many life strategies, all with the intention of making us feel better, that do just the opposite. It's not anyone's fault, per se; it's just that we have forgotten what our goal is and how we can get there. By using the criterion of whether something makes us feel good or not we can create valuable and realistic pleasure strategies for ourselves.

Often enough, if we want to get the most pleasure out of something, we have to endure or experience something we regard as painful first. For example, if I want to continue to enjoy my house in this neighborhood, I will have to pay the property taxes on it. I will also have to pay a great many other bills to allow me this pleasure. But the overall satisfaction of living in my house is well worth it.

If I want to earn enough money to spend my vacations in Hawaii, then I may have to spend the time and money to go to school first and learn a vocation that pays well. If I want to feel free from all my anxieties, then I will first have to feel all the hurt and angry feelings that I have avoided for years.

The point is that using pleasure as a guide doesn't mean we never have to experience painful things again. It means that when we remember that we are trying to feel as good as possible we need to determine which things we can avoid and which things we have to experience before we can have the pleasurable experiences we're looking for.

To understand how to use pleasure as a guide, we must first understand the power of pleasure.

In India, there is a lovely tree called *Parijat*. Botanically, it's called *Nyctanthis arbor-tristes*. But another name for this tree is *The Wish-Fulfilling Tree*. It is a medium-sized tree with lots of delicate honey-scented flowers. It has such a divine fragrance that it is said that smelling it brings forth the power to have one's wishes immediately manifest.

The story goes that one time a traveler in India who had been walking for a long time found a Parijat tree that looked very agreeable to sit under and rest. After catching his breath for a few moments, he said gently, "My legs are so tired; I wish I had someone to massage them for me." And instantly a young woman appeared and set about massaging his tired legs. When his legs felt better, and the massage was over he noticed that he was very hungry. "Oh, I wish I had some food to eat." No sooner were his words spoken than before him appeared a great feast. Many of his favorite dishes were within arm's reach. He eagerly started eating his fill and enjoying this great bounty.

When he was finished, he became drowsy and decided to take a nap. As he was getting comfortable for his sleep, he fearfully said, "Oh, I hope a tiger doesn't come now and eat me up!" And, of course, a tiger immediately appeared and had a great feast of its own!

Pleasure is very powerful in its own right!

For starters, our bodies are exquisitely designed for pleasure. All of our senses react to what we like and what we don't like. The body needs pleasure on a regular basis, just like any other nutrient. Without daily pleasures, the body becomes numb and becomes unresponsive to the world around it. A happy body is much less likely to get sick or feel pain.

When we experience pleasure, we relax, and our bodies function the way they were intended to. On the other hand, when we tense up in fear or pain we constrict the body's functioning in preparation for dealing with some threat. This "on alert" status means that energy and nutrients are distributed differently, and we live in the moment differently.

Our minds are also designed for pleasure. We do things mentally to feel good, like solving problems, accomplishing things, and overcoming challenges. If our minds don't get to do things they like, they will rebel. They will grow bored and do other things, like daydreaming or getting angry.

And, of course, our emotions and feelings are all about pleasure. So pleasure is the name of the game. It is what our lives are all about, whether we want to acknowledge that or not.

I want to be very clear here that not all pleasures are self-indulgent. One of the greatest joys I know of is that of being of service to others. Compassion, the urge to help relieve the suffering of others, is also a pleasure, albeit one that also includes the feelings of those we want to help. Quietly sitting and being present to oneself can be an immense pleasure. In fact, being present, even to one's own sorrows, is usually experienced as a pleasure. And simple friendship is one of the greatest pleasures we can know.

To maximize our pleasures we need to have a good idea of what we want. Most of us have desires to do, be, or have something. There's nothing wrong with having desires. However, we need to look underneath each of our desires and find the feeling that is the basis of our desire. We want to experience one or more specific feelings. Understanding those foundational feelings that we desire often makes the "thing" that we wanted unnecessary.

For example, some years ago I wanted a sailboat because I wanted to experience the exquisite feeling of freedom that comes from sailing in front of the wind on a beautiful day. A few years later, I wanted to sell that same sailboat so that I could experience the exquisite feeling of freedom, getting rid of the expense and hassle of owning a boat. It was the same *feeling* that I wanted, that of freedom. If we understand that it actually is the feeling of freedom, for example, that we want, we can make other, less expensive choices to get that feeling.

Our pleasure is a direct result of what we are focusing on, plain and simple. Focus on our misery brings more misery. Focusing on our enjoyment and pleasure brings us more joy and pleasure. Focusing on all the things that need to be done often overlooks the fact that all those things that need to be done are necessary in order to experience more pleasure. If we're not taking the time to enjoy the fruits of our labors thoroughly then, why bother doing those labors?

However, it's important to remember that all pleasures come to an end. That's the nature of pleasure. When we can hold the understanding that *all* pleasures will cease at some point, we can prepare ourselves for the inevitable. The idea that something we love will continue forever can cripple us when the unavoidable moment comes when what we've been enjoying comes to an end. If we are unprepared, our belief about the perpetual enjoyment of that something will be dashed.

However, that doesn't mean that our inner joy comes to an end. One way of looking at happiness is that it is moving gracefully from one pleasure to the next. By taking into account the transitory nature of pleasure we can enjoy things while we can and inoculate ourselves against the pain of a pleasure concluded. We can only be happy right now, knowing that things will change. We can put off pleasures in this moment with the anticipation of greater pleasures later. But putting off happiness is merely wasting happiness. We can be happy anytime we choose by being present to ourselves and whatever is happening right now.

To experience the things and people we love is to be happy with them. That is, we enjoy them, we appreciate them, we have fun with them, and we find pleasure in them. Criticism, judgment, and shame all destroy the pleasure of the things and the people we love. So when we look at anything or anyone with any sense that they are not as perfect as we think they should be, we are relinquishing our happiness and the pleasure of that moment. When we allow ourselves to enjoy whatever is happening to the highest degree possible, we bask in the ocean of love.

This is the heart of accomplishment because pleasure is the measure of success. Since our motivation has been feeling good in whatever we've chosen to do, reaching our goal is gaining the pleasure from the achievement. When we take responsibility for the degree of pleasure, joy, and happiness in our lives we hold the keys to success in our hands. We make the choices for our happiness. And when we have decided for ourselves that we choose happiness, then all of our decisions become based on whether or not these choices add to or detract from our overall happiness.

Are we getting enough enjoyment, pleasure, love, accomplishment, or happiness out of what we are doing and how we do it? That is, does what we're doing actually work for us? This is an invitation to look over our lives and examine whether or not we are truly enjoying our lives as we might. Are we doing things that seem like good ideas but that are actually draining our energy and sapping our pleasure instead? Perhaps it is time to look at our lives so that we can nurture the joys and weed out all those unnecessary miseries.

All too often I have encountered people who appreciate pleasure and feeling good when they occur but who feel the need to make sure that all the other important things are taken care of first. It's as though feeling good was the reward for doing things well or "right," and one needed to keep pushing forward in hope of finally getting to the point of enjoyment.

These people miss a crucial point: working within the context of pleasure, that is, feeling good to begin with, is how a person can be most effective. Pleasure is both the reward and the key element in living a constructive life. By maintaining a sense of feeling good, we can retain and develop the power we need to do the things we want to do.

There Are Many Ways that Pleasure Is Powerful

Our energy is highest when we are enjoying ourselves. When we have more energy we can accomplish more. We put our *hearts* into it. Since we are always motivated to do things that will help us feel better, the better the feeling, the higher the motivation (to the degree that we don't resist ourselves.) As Dale Carnegie said, "People rarely succeed unless they have fun in what they are doing."

If I am enjoying the task I am involved in, I don't notice the time passing. I get into a kind of "flow state" that is very productive and fun. But this flow state is only achievable if I am enjoying what I'm doing.

Think of a time in your life when you were relishing what you were doing and accomplished it easily. Now think of a time recently when you had a task to do that you weren't enthusiastic about doing. Notice the difference in your ability to do those things.

The trick here is to see if you can find the pleasure in the task you weren't enthusiastic about carrying out. The pleasure would probably have been in enjoying the results of your efforts. Changing your perspective might have changed your response to the task you weren't enjoying at first.

As the late, great teacher, Mary Poppins, said:

In every job that must be done,
There is an element of fun.
You find the fun, and the job's a game.

Pleasure is a sign that most or all of us are in alignment with what we are doing and thus we are not losing energy by fighting ourselves. When we are enjoying ourselves we are in the present moment. We can only enjoy something in the present when we can let go of doubt and fear. So often we let concerns about what other people are thinking, or how we should be doing something intrude, and as a result we allow some of the pleasure to slip away.

Many people think of pain as being the opposite of pleasure. They are indeed on the same spectrum. But fear is the real opposite of pleasure. Fear shuts down pleasure and keeps us from feeling the lovely effects of pleasure. When we let go of fear we automatically start feeling good again. By choosing to pay attention to our fears and doubts, we suck the energy right out of us. On the other hand, when we stay in the present moment and enjoy it, appreciating the simple elements of our lives, our fears fade away.

We are most effective when we are resonating fully with what we want to accomplish. When we praise, bless, or appreciate the thing we are looking for or want to do, we come into a kind of vibrational alignment with it. If we want to manifest something we do it by enjoying in the present moment what it is we fancy. We give thanks for it now, to be in the vibration of what it is we desire.

Make it a habit of telling people "thank you." Express your appreciation sincerely and without the expectation of anything in return. Truly appreciate those around you, and you'll soon find many others around you. Truly appreciate life, and you'll find that you have more of it.
Ralph Marston

Here's a simple way of demonstrating this. On a scale of 1 to 10, how would you rate the level of your vibration right now, with 10 being the very highest? That is, subjectively estimate how good you feel. This is a rough measure of your vibration. Now spend the next minute, 60 seconds, appreciating things that you can see from where you sit. When you have finished appreciating things for one minute, how would you rate your vibration using that same scale? You are very likely to feel a substantial difference.

This book is not ostensibly about magic. Yet there is a definite magic in feeling good and sharing that beautiful feeling state with others. Things happen easily, coincidences appear, synchronicities abound, and life seems much less complicated.

We influence parts of the world around us when we connect to them. We relate by feeling good and appreciating them or praising them. That's why gods and influential people are always approached with gifts and compliments—to connect with them and influence them favorably. Nagging and criticizing are seldom effective because they exist in the absence of connection. However, when we find some way of feeling good with someone or about something, we have opened our hearts and established some relationship in which to operate.

We all know the effectiveness of smiling when we want to influence someone to do something that is favorable to us. Frowning, which is showing our displeasure, doesn't get us anything but a chilly reception. A smile shows that we are feeling good and lets other people resonate with our good feeling.

When we are experiencing pleasure we are connected to our deepest core, our Higher Mind, or High Self. Whatever we call the non-physical parts of ourselves, it is from these places that we have access to inspiration and insight in abundance. Thus, pleasure stimulates creativity. The sexy little Greek Muses were inspirational because they stimulated pleasure.

Try feeling inward for inspiration when you feel stress. You won't get much inspiration. But when you relax and can enjoy the moment all your questions can be answered, and ideas will flow naturally.

As we learn more about who we truly are and get in touch with our center, we quickly notice how good that feels. And when we let go of our center and get further and further away from it we can easily see how bad it feels. Thus, pleasure, that sense of feeling good, is our guiding star by which we can steer.

Here's a little opportunity to experience this. Sit quietly now, and enjoy the pleasure of breathing easily. Nothing needs to be done. Just relax. Now, silently ask a question you'd like the answer to. You don't have to be clear about who you're asking. Just see what pops into your mind after you ask the question. If nothing comes into your mind try relaxing even more, and try again.

Since feeling good is the best definition we have of health, it is what we want for those in need of healing. We can be most effective when we offer the highest vibration we can hold in ourselves for others to resonate with for their own healing. We allow them to "tune into" our stronger and more powerful vibration of pleasure. Besides, when we hold the vibration of good health and happiness with others in mind, we also reap the benefits for ourselves.

When we want to help someone emotionally we often "send" them love. But to have something to send, we have to be in a place of love. If we are feeling hurt or resentful, what we have to send is only hurt and resentment. Feeling our pleasure as fully as possible gives us something substantial to send to others and for them to resonate with.

Here's another little experience for you. Sit quietly and relax all your muscles. Scan your whole body several times and see if you can find other muscles to relax. Now scan your emotional body, your feelings, and discover where you may be tensing up, and see if you can intentionally relax those places. Now watch your thoughts, and consciously set aside any thoughts that bring tension into your life. You can look at these later; but for now, let them fade into the background. And let go of all of your needs to be in control. You can have preferences, but you aren't in full control.

Now feel the flow of life energy coursing through you. You might want to picture it flowing up your central core, coming out your head, and spiraling down to your feet to flow through you again. Or you may merely feel a pulsing glow. You may experience it entirely differently, but you are likely to experience some sense of life energy within your being. Take some time to luxuriate in this delicious feeling, and get to know it thoroughly. Then, whenever you want to return to this feeling, you can just summon the memory of this experience.

Pleasure gives us a standard by which we can make our choices and organize our plans. It is in being aware of what makes us feel the best that we can choose those things to do, be, or have that will maximize our pleasure, love, and joy. As we've seen, pleasure is our spiritual guidance system. Once we learn to use that system on a regular basis our lives become immeasurably easier and happier.

Pleasure is like a currency, like the dollar or the euro. We quickly judge which of our choices will likely give us the most pleasure and that is the one we desire the most. So by understanding that we are actually judging what will bring us pleasure, we can think with our hearts in making important decisions.

This is an important idea to hold onto. If we are not aware of how we are making our choices we will overlook the effect these beginning assumptions have on those choices. Choosing on the basis of fear will give us inspirations and options for diminishing fear, but nothing more. Deciding on the basis of joy and pleasure will provide us with inspirations and options for adding more joy and pleasure to our lives. We will get radically different options and probabilities depending on how we frame our choice.

Think about something you have to make a decision on soon. It could be something trivial or something significant; it doesn't matter. Now, think of this decision from the perspective of some of the nasty things that might happen if you don't make the right choice. Focus on that result for just a moment and see how it feels.

Now think of your impending decision on the basis of the benefits and pleasure you will get if you make a good decision. See if you can determine which choice will give you the maximum amount of pleasure. See how that feels and notice the difference in the two ways of thinking.

An awareness of your level of pleasure is the foundation of your communication with your body. As we said before, our body is designed for pleasure. It wants to avoid pain and move toward pleasure; that's what it is most interested in. To find out what is bothering the body we need to ask, "Where is the pain?" and "Where is the pain coming from?"

Since our bodies are primarily focused on pleasure, when something hurts we start looking for what will make us feel good again. Talking to our body is the first place to start. We want to know, from the body's point of view, what's happening that shouldn't be. We may get answers that we don't like, such as "I'm tired, and I don't want to do this anymore!" Or, "I don't want to be here now!" There is more to us than just our bodies, of course. But unless the body is happy, the rest of us can never be happy.

I suggest that you ask your body right now what you could do to give it more pleasure. Scan your body to find ways to make it more comfortable. For example, would your body like some water? Would your body like to take a nap? Is your body yearning for something sweet or maybe some coffee? Is there something hurting in your body, or perhaps something is simply tense? What can you do to make your body happier? Notice how your body responds to being asked about its pleasure.

Let me remind you why pleasure is so important.

It is the motivation we have to do anything.
It is the sense of excitement about being alive.
It gives life meaning and purpose.
It is calming and thus reduces stress and promotes health.
It is the currency with which we evaluate our future activities.
Pleasure is the measure of success.

Pleasure raises our vibration and thus makes us more effective in whatever we are doing. Pleasure doesn't just change us; it changes the energy around us, and that influences other people. If we can raise the vibration of others around us, that effect can spread around the world.

Letting go of the petty annoyances, missed expectations, and little hurts, and focusing on what makes us feel good brings joy to the world and thus aids in bringing peace to us all.

I want to finish this chapter with our friend under the Parijat tree. He had a partial understanding of the power of pleasure, but he didn't have the skill to maintain his focus. He realized that when he felt especially good his very being could powerfully manifest his desires. But he neglected, or didn't understand, that this same power could make his fears manifest with equal ease.

When we keep our focus on what makes us feel good and stimulates our joy, we greatly increase our creativity and effectiveness. When we remember why we are doing anything, that is, we do it to feel good, we keep our power without dissipating it.

We all have an extraordinary source of power within us. The question isn't, "Is it there or not?"; it is definitely there. The questions are, how are we going to access that power and how will we use it? That's what the next chapters are all about.

And the next meditation is about how we can use our focus and love to assist our bodies as they go through the natural process of coming back into wholeness.

Meditation 4
Helping My Body Heal

I've done everything I need to do at this time. Everything is taken care of, for now. Now it's time for me to relax and heal. My body is trying to solve a problem, and I want to help it in any way I can. I know I can start helping by just relaxing. I allow myself to relax and breathe easily.

My body is my friend, and my friend needs help. Just as with any dear friend, I treat my body with deep love, respect, and honor. My body has been through a lot, and I hope it will continue to thrive for a long time to come. I want it to become healthy again very quickly.

I see some of the ways that I may have been creating stress in my body. I have been carrying a lot of tension, and it doesn't have to be this way. I can let go of some of this stress. For the sake of my health, I think I will let go of some of my stress and anxiety.

It feels good to let go of stress. It really doesn't do me any good, anyway. I know my body heals faster when I'm relaxed. So I relax and let my tensions slip away. I like the feeling of relaxing. I love the feeling of peace. I like the feeling of being very calm.

I choose to believe that there are unseen helpers who are ready to help me, if I will only ask. So I ask them now for help. I ask that this infirmity that I'm experiencing dissolve away. I ask that I be assisted in returning to full health.

There is love and light all around me and I let it in. I let the light seep into every cell of my body. I let the light energize all the elements of my body that are working to correct this imbalance. I let the light fill me with hope, fill me with love, and fill me with compassion for the suffering of others.

I let all toxic negativity drain away. I don't mean to be critical or judgmental. It just pops out. But I know it doesn't serve me. I know it makes me tense. So I let it go. I allow it to fall away from me like dead skin and cut hair. I let all my negativity drain away.

I love my body. I love how it responds so readily to my will. I love how it feels in the sunlight. I love how it feels with a little exercise. I love how it feels in a bath or shower. I love how it feels when I've eaten an excellent meal. My body is a great wonder of the universe. What a magical and amazing gift this body is!

There probably are some lessons for me to learn here. I probably can use these lessons to stay away from this infirmity in the future. I can probably learn to be wiser from this experience. There probably are even some reasons to be grateful here today.

I picture my body as a little child in my arms. I hold it with all the love and affection I can. I rock it to sleep gently at night and guard it carefully. I nurture my body with kindness, tenderness, and a deep understanding of all that is happening to it right now.

I am here for my body. I am ready to help it however I can. I love my body, and I want to show that love every minute of every day. This healing will be complete soon, and I am very grateful for that. And the love that grows because of this experience will serve me for the rest of my life.

*The ultimate authority must always rest
with the individual's own reason and critical analysis.*
The Dalai Lama

Chapter 5

Getting Lost in Criticism

There is a pervasive notion in the world that criticizing people, including ourselves, is a necessary part of life. The idea is that our faults and the faults of others need to be pointed out to make people better. A simple consideration of how much criticism is doled out each day versus the amount of change we can see shows us how ineffective all of this criticism is. If it worked, we would have created a worldwide utopia long ago. Making our way home to ourselves involves identifying and choosing how to respond to the many traps that criticism presents us with. So let's look at criticism a little closer.

To begin with, nobody likes to be criticized. And most of us have had so much experience of being criticized and being made to feel small and unworthy that we will do almost anything to avoid it. This fear of being criticized then takes hold deep within us and starts to cripple us as we step out into the world, afraid of what the world might say to or about us.

This fear is such a hot button for many people that it triggers anger and resentment immediately. For some people, it even generates rage. People feel personally attacked and will do whatever it takes to fend that off.

But wouldn't it be nice if we could easily neutralize criticism and not let the fear of being criticized affect us?

The first thing to remember is that a criticism is only someone else's opinion. That is to say, it's just a reflection of what's happening inside them that they are projecting on to us. Perhaps there's something useful in what they're saying, but most of it is really about them.

We're not here to be responsible for how other people feel, especially about how they feel about what we're doing or how we do it. We are only accountable for how *we* feel. If we start being responsible for how others feel, we'll never have time for anything else. Besides, it disempowers them when we do it. If we're taking care of other peoples' feelings for them, we take away their power to choose what they want to feel at any given time.

The second thing is that they base their criticism on values, perceptions and perspectives that we don't necessarily have to agree with. If we're being criticized for continually wearing Hawaiian Aloha shirts, the person criticizing us may well be lacking an appreciation for the comfort, beauty, and level of "cool" that is inherent in these shirts. We may be criticized for being messy which reflects more about the other person's preference than ours. We may be criticized for procrastinating, which may overlook our need to take the time to fully feel our way into the task at hand and what it requires from us.

We make our choices based on what seems best for us at that moment. That's the best any of us can do. The trick here is to trust ourselves to know what's best for us. Actually, we don't even have to know what's best; we just need to be okay with experimenting.

As mentioned earlier, each act we make is an effort to feel better than we did in the previous moment. There's no reason for us to expect to do everything "right" or "perfect." That's not the point of life. Life is a glorious adventure in which we explore lots of things.

The third thing to remember is that we aren't really supposed to know everything. We're often criticized as kids for not "knowing better," even if that's the first time we encountered that particular situation or problem. We often grow up with a sense that somewhere along the line there must have been a manual that tells us everything we're supposed to know and somehow we lost that manual along the way.

If you haven't already sorted it out, there *never* was such a manual. And, in fact, those who criticize us for not knowing something had to have had someone else tell them, show them, or they figured it out at some cost to themselves at some point.

So we end up with a fear of criticism based on the idea that somehow we are mysteriously supposed to know how to do things—and to do them correctly. Failing to do these things the right way means that we are defective in some way. This is a form of insanity. We're not capable of knowing everything and the way we learn is through making "mistakes." Being afraid of making mistakes means that we are afraid of learning.

When we look at how criticism works, we can see that it primarily makes us feel bad about ourselves. This is the essence of hell. So the skill of neutralizing the fear of criticism is two-fold. One, it is about knowing how to defuse the effects of criticism. And two, it's about knowing that we can get out of hell easily any time we need to.

Criticism works its insidious black magic by making us focus on aspects of ourselves that we don't particularly like. It would have absolutely no effect if it didn't resonate with some belief we already have. If someone snidely says to us that we look just like every other human in the world, then we're probably not going to get upset. We are likely to be okay with looking more or less like most other humans. There's no central negative belief to resonate with. If, however, that person snidely says that we're an *ugly* human being, it will bother us to the degree that we aren't happy with how we look.

If we find that certain criticisms get to us, that's a signal that we have some specific work to do. Fear of criticism may well mean that we are very reluctant to face something in particular. Whenever we get angry at a criticism, it reveals to us that we are experiencing a negative self-belief that is in alignment with the criticism. Part of us believes what is being said.

Facing that something and feeling the feelings associated with that something is the fastest way to get it out of our system. We feel it and change our belief to something more positive. If we go through that process fully, no criticism on that score will ever hurt again.

So there are a few choices you can make when someone criticizes you.

The first one is to change your focus. You can remember something you like about yourself, such as your sense of humor, your taste in clothes, or your ability to care about others. Remembering whatever you like about yourself will help you feel good about yourself, and that's where your power lies.

Another thing to do is to say, "Thank you" or "Thanks. I'll consider that," even when the criticism is said with anger. I particularly like this because it pretends that the person doing the criticizing was just trying to do us a favor, and it usually shuts them up. People often want to put their own personal pain on to us. When you accept the criticism without otherwise reacting, that leaves them to deal with their own feelings.

Another thing to remember is, there are no points to lose if you make a mistake. If someone is losing respect for you based on the mistakes you've made, then they have forgotten all the many mistakes they've made. Reminding them of that may make them mad, but reminding yourself of it can bring you back to a healthy perspective.

Now we get to the heart of the problem—hell. As we discussed at the beginning, criticism can make us feel genuinely miserable. It can lead us to dwell on our shortcomings and failures. And it can make us feel like there is no hope we will ever "get it right."

So here are some points to remember so that you don't ever have to be afraid of your own hell again. The most important thing is to recognize that you put yourself there, with your thoughts, your beliefs, and your desires. They all contributed to the feelings you have that bring you so far down that you can accurately call it hell. However, if you put yourself there, you can take yourself out, too.

Also, recognize that hell is the continuous focus on things that displease you greatly. You feel that negativity in every part of your being. When you're in hell, it seems like there is no way out. It is the overwhelming feeling of helplessness and hopelessness.

The first step to coming out of hell is to find some feeling that feels better than helplessness. Anger generally feels better. So does a desire for revenge. Hope feels much better, if you can reach that high. There's no need to judge the better feeling as not being good enough. If it makes you feel a little better, then you're on your way.

As you start to feel even a little bit better, intentionally find things that you enjoy. Perhaps a piece of music, a flower, the memory of someone you loved, or a favorite smell. Let your focus rest on the pleasant feeling that you're experiencing. As we discussed in Chapter 3, you have the power to move your focus all around and choose where it will come to rest. Focusing on the things that make you feel unhappy will only increase that unhappiness. If there are things that need to be done to return your focus to the things that you enjoy, then take care of them as quickly as possible.

There may well be feelings that need to be felt fully in order to let them go. And these feelings may seem overwhelming and confusing to handle. However, it is only by going through them that you can get out the other side. You may also need to relax into the intensity of the feeling. *Remember, your feelings can't hurt you, but resisting them can.*

The **fear** of hell can be debilitating all by itself. Often this fear is much worse than the actual experience of feeling bad (depressed, deeply remorseful, despairing, miserable, melancholic). But when we know how to get out of our hell, should we find that we have fallen into it, we don't need to be afraid. We don't need to linger in hell any longer than it takes to notice that that's where we are and that we don't want to be there any longer.

So, when we look at why we are afraid of criticism, we can see that nasty feelings are lurking around the corner that we don't want to face. Having confidence that we can handle those ugly feelings makes criticism just another experience that we need to deal with quickly, like taking out the garbage or mowing the lawn. Pure self-love is the very best antidote to criticism. Remembering that you know how to deal with criticism is a marvelous act of self-love.

In the next few chapters, we will look at several of the specific ways that we hurt ourselves. In fact, we are downright cruel, treating ourselves much worse than those we say we don't like. Most of the things we do to ourselves come under the heading of shame.

As was mentioned earlier, shame is the choice to disapprove of ourselves in some way. It is saying that there is something wrong with us, that there is something that needs fixing. It is the non-acceptance of our full being. None of us has escaped from having this experience, though some have mostly worked their way out of it. And, to make matters worse, nobody wants to admit that they have shame. We're ashamed of our shame. That makes shame very difficult to look at.

To begin with, we need to admit and accept that we feel shame. It may show up about parts of our body that we hide from others. It may lurk in how we feel about our intelligence or our physical abilities. It may center on our social standing or our financial situation. It could show up in how tightly we control our sexual feelings and urges. It may surround experiences that we have had that made us victims. Perhaps we even had conflicting feelings in the course of being victims.

Guilt is the choice to disapprove of something we've done. That's a different phenomenon. The feeling is often similar to that of shame, but it works differently. The antidote to guilt is forgiveness. That's a process that is reasonably straight-forward. Getting past shame is a much bigger operation.

Essentially, shame is the opposite of self-love. It says that some part or parts of us can't be loved as they are. Since just about everybody walks around with aspects of themselves that they don't like or love, we are all experiencing shame on a regular basis. It doesn't have to be that way. But dealing with that shame is the essence of coming home to ourselves. It is shame that keeps us outside of our home, cold and lonely.

The idea that there is something not right with us is a belief that comes from elsewhere, outside of us. We can't decide that there's something wrong with us without comparing ourselves to something or someone else unfavorably. Generally, we are encouraged to make that comparison so that we can become "better human beings." The question of *why* we need to be better seldom arises.

Compassion for ourselves means accepting each and every aspect of our existence. This attitude is the opposite of shame. Being compassionate becomes a matter of sifting through the myriad beliefs we have taken on about how we *should* be but are not. We can't find our way home while we still think that we don't belong there.

What do we do about shame?

Whenever someone criticizes you, or you criticize yourself, find something to shift your focus to that makes you feel good, especially things that make you feel good about yourself. Instead of, "What was I thinking?" ask yourself, "What was I learning?" Instead of, "That was dumb of me!" tell yourself, "I understand better now!"

It really doesn't matter what we shift our focus to as long as it is positive. What works is the change of focus itself. A criticism of some part of us, or something we've done, tends to hijack our focus to align with someone else's ideas. When we reclaim our focus, we're back on an even keel.

Actively and intentionally choose to love yourself as you are. This choice is part self-acceptance and part awareness of what your current experience is. As part of this, it's helpful to choose to discover who you are in your entirety. I believe that we, as a species, are changing and that there is a substantial shift of consciousness occurring. And I think that this work of choosing to discover and accept who we are is the keystone of this shift.

Choose to identify yourself as Spirit, or a union of body, mind and Spirit. Some people go for learning to believe that they are God—"I am God." That works nicely if you genuinely believe it. By identifying yourself as Spirit, you acknowledge that *you are a divine being no matter what!* Nothing can change that no matter what you do or what you are. This perspective is also useful as you move into accepting your full potential as a human being.

If you are still aware of shame within yourself, look at your belief system, your operating system, and ask, "What idea or belief do I continue to have in my operating system that causes me to feel shame?" Choose new beliefs that make you feel supremely good about yourself. Sit with those new beliefs now, and remind yourself of them from time to time until you have fully integrated them into your own personal belief system.

As you learn to love yourself consistently, things that you have previously been unaware of are likely to appear—new fears, shames, or doubts. This is normal. They are merely all those things that you have not been ready to deal with in the past. Now they are coming up to be seen and dispensed with. You will return to the wonderful space of loving yourself just as soon as you've conquered these.

When criticism gets complicated

Whenever I find myself responding to someone's request for help, one of the main points I emphasize is the need to stop criticizing—in any fashion. Any form of criticism beyond critiquing, as in works of art, is harmful. It doesn't matter whether the criticism is of oneself or someone else; effectively, they are the same thing. Not only does criticism harm the person giving it, criticism also sends out a very low vibration that encourages others to resonate with that lower vibration; it brings them down emotionally as well.

However, what happens when we encounter situations where there are one or more people who have very powerful negative vibrations, as in anger or fear, and with whom we must interact on a regular basis? We are aware that being around them brings our energy down. To express our displeasure with them in any way is a criticism. On the other hand, to ignore our dissatisfaction with the situation is to do emotional violence to ourselves. So, how do we resolve this?

The answer lies in how we can best keep our vibration up while both taking care of ourselves, and the situation in which we find ourselves. I see three parts to this.

The first thing is to hold our focus on the things we like. Gratitude works well for this and helps us to maintain the fundamental vibration we want to live in. This doesn't mean ignoring anything. It simply is taking some time to remember how beautiful things are, for the most part. We might say that this is the background vibration or the context in which we will solve our problems.

The second step is to do something, anything, which makes us feel we are actively addressing the current challenge. This task may involve trying to make peace with the person who challenges us. It may require us to look for ways to distance ourselves from this person. Or we may need to consciously change the vibration around the whole room, office, building or city where this dissonance is occurring. This kind of intentional vibrational shift is just a matter of holding some intention for harmony or peace and finding a suitable symbol for that intention, like a fog of pleasantly colored goodwill or fairies dusting the whole area with joy, and then repeating and visualizing that intention on a regular basis.

The third step is to look at what this situation is showing us. How is this challenge teaching us something about ourselves? For instance, we could be facing the problem of a coworker who never stops complaining. This coworker may see him or herself consistently as a victim, and that victimhood has become such a part of their identity that no suggestions to the contrary will have any effect. What might this situation be teaching us about our own beliefs about victimhood?

How we react to this person is our choice. We can be invested in anger, disgust, sadness, or all three. Or we could choose something else. We could choose to react with pity and ignore the person while

It's Time to Come Home

holding on to an idea that he or she is pathetic. We could choose to say to ourselves, "This person was put on my path to show me something and I'll look for that lesson in this situation." We might even choose to bless the person for driving home to us the importance of keeping our vibration as high as possible so that we don't end up just like that person.

Plenty of situations occur where we don't understand how we are responsible for their occurrence, at least not right away. But we are responsible for all of our reactions to those situations. Choosing the one with the highest vibration will keep us the happiest.

So how does that relate to criticism? At the most basic level, criticism brings us down and is a poor choice if we are choosing to be as happy as possible. However, at a more complex level, we need to acknowledge that some things are not working for us. We are unhappy or dissatisfied with something in our current situation. It is at this moment, the moment when we realize our displeasure, that we can use these feelings to motivate us to change things. Yes, it is a criticism to say, "I don't like that!" And holding this feeling will start to make us sick. But, if we can take charge, use our power, and begin immediately looking for a better way, we can transform our objection into the seed for a new reality. This approach is the empowered way to deal with challenges. But without using our dissatisfaction immediately, we wallow in the negativity.

So the trick here is to be very conscious of how we handle the things we don't like. It is quite natural to not like some things, to no longer like some things, and even to never want to get close enough to like or dislike some things. What we need to do is to change our focus as fast as we can without ignoring problems where we can do something. And there is always *something* we can do. We do that something as efficiently as we can, and then move back into our joy. We swiftly get out of the energy of criticism and let it catapult us into a much better space.

And remember, the most powerful thing we can do in life is to be happy!

Here's a little exercise to help you work with this. Just try to speculate on the following questions.

How often each day do you criticize yourself for something you've done or haven't done? These could be little criticisms along the lines of not accomplishing everything you set out to do or forgetting an item on your shopping list to more significant things like not living up to your parents' ideas of who you should be by now or putting on a few too many pounds. Just see if you can get an idea of how often you say things to yourself about how you didn't do things right.

Now, how often each day do you do things to avoid being criticized yourself? These are the things about not wanting to disappoint other people or thinking that they will speak poorly of you if you don't do certain things.

How often each day do you get annoyed when others don't do what you expected them to do? Again, these could be little things like a waitress forgetting to get you more coffee to a neighbor playing music too loudly. This awareness is a matter of seeing how your judgments of others affect you emotionally.

How often each day do you tell stories about your life in which you were abused, hurt, demeaned, ignored, put upon, or otherwise victimized? Each time you share your version of your history in a way that depicts how you suffered, notice how it makes you feel.

How often each day do you worry about what's going to happen to you or to those you love? Some worries seem to make sense because you want to make sure that the nasty things don't happen. At other times worries probably loop in your head, and you imagine unfortunate things happening again and again.

How often each day do you regret things that have happened? Do you remember things in your past, either recent or long ago, and genuinely wish things had gone differently? These are the particulars of your life that just don't fit in comfortably. Perhaps you have only one or two things like this; maybe you have many. Whichever it is, here are aspects of your life that you have not yet come to terms with.

How often each day do you feel ashamed of some aspect of who you are? These are the things that don't seem to align with what you think is normal or right. Every time you think of how things would be better if only you were a little different you are expressing shame.

And how often each day do you feel guilty about something you've done or haven't done? Are there things niggling in the recesses of your mind that cause you discomfort? These are the guilty feelings that show you that you are not in alignment with what you think you should have done.

By remembering that we are actively seeking to feel better in all we do, we can then be compassionate with ourselves each time we encounter one of these challenges. We don't have to beat ourselves up. We don't have to find fault with ourselves. We don't have to say nasty things about any aspect of ourselves. We just need to accept that whatever it is or was has had some reality, but we don't need to dwell on it and we don't need to make it a part of how we create our future.

The point of letting go of our criticisms, our feelings of shame, and our feelings of guilt is to keep our focus on the possibilities that are in front of us. With the past comfortably behind us, we can make new decisions about what happens next without a heavy cloud of judgments. Each moment can be a fresh start that isn't dependent on the moments that came before.

Meditation 5
I Love Feeling Peaceful

What a sweet pleasure it is to breathe, just to breathe easily and fully. I like feeling my chest expanding and contracting. I love how my breath deepens when I relax. I like the extra relaxation I feel when I exhale. I feel at peace with being alive when my breathing is relaxed. I love breathing.

I like feeling better, and I like the pleasure of relaxing. Relaxing is such a big pleasure all by itself. Each muscle that relaxes makes me feel even better. I like telling specific muscles to relax and feeling the pleasure when they do. I like letting all my muscles relax.

I enjoy just being in the present moment. When there is nothing I am willing to worry about, and nothing that I let disturb me from the past, I simply take pleasure in being right here, right now. The tranquility of this moment is delicious.

When I am present to myself, I see more clearly, hear more clearly, and everything around me seems brighter and more vital. I like that. There is a particular sense of aliveness in being in the moment that feels especially good.

I enjoy being at peace with the Earth. This fantastic planet that I live on nurtures me beautifully when I let it. When I am at peace with the Earth, I can feel her raw beauty, and I know that, in time, she will right any imbalances. I *love doing my part to take care of her, just as she takes care of me. I love the Earth.*

It feels so good when I am at peace with the people around me. I much prefer to let the little things go, so that I can enjoy my peace. My peace is so important to me that I am willing to ignore and overlook many things that I used to let bother me. I really like my peace.

I love being at peace with my body. My body is my friend, my very dear friend. And just like any dear friend, I avoid criticizing my body whenever I can. My body likes it when I compliment it. And I like it, too, when I compliment my body.

My body likes it when I tell it I'm grateful for all the excellent work it does. I like making my body happy. When my body is happy, I am happy. I love my body, as I know it loves me.

I love being at peace with my past. It's all over now; the past is just memories of experiences. Some of them I liked and some I didn't like. But now those experiences have faded into the background of my life. I don't have to hang on to painful memories any more than I have to remember a stubbed toe. I make peace with my past by merely allowing those memories to exist in their own world, and I let the hard feelings about them dissolve away. I love the peace of forgiveness.

I love being at peace with my future. I don't know what will happen next, and that's okay. I know I will do the best I can, and that's enough. I know that when I relax and stay in a place of feeling good, things always seem to work out for me. I enjoy my desires for new experiences, and I let them unfold in their own time. I love the peace of trust.

I love being at peace with myself. Whatever this amazing being that I call "me" is, I think it's wonderful. I know that I don't have to be anything other than who I am. No one else's ideas of who I should be are nearly as important as how I really am. I enjoy discovering new things about myself. And I appreciate the new ways that I recreate myself each day. I love being me. I love being alive. And I love being at peace with myself.

*The greatest discovery of any generation is that human beings
can alter their lives by altering the attitudes of their minds.*
Albert Schweitzer

Chapter 6

Mastering Expectation

Expectations are strange creatures. They have a life of their own that has the ability to affect how our lives play out. When we use them with skill and awareness, they help us focus our energies to accomplish the great things we strive for.

When not used correctly, though, an expectation can be one of the most fiendish forms of self-torture. Expectation is the belief that something, in particular, is definitely going to happen. And, in fact, we are so confident in our expectation that we eliminate all doubt about what's coming. That's what makes it so powerful if used appropriately, and that's also why it gets us into trouble. If we expect something to happen and it doesn't happen, then we generally default to disappointment and feel unhappy.

But we are the ones who create expectations. They aren't laws of nature; they are tools for organizing our future. Sometimes they are used retroactively, as in expecting our parents to have done things differently when we were younger. But that is a particularly twisted way of saying that we wish things had been different, and then blaming people who were doing the best they knew how for things they couldn't have foreseen. Usually, though, we expect things based on our current desires. We imagine how something wonderful will be, and in that anticipation we create an image that we expect to appear. Imagination is a magnificent implement for designing our future, but the added step of expecting needs to be done consciously and wisely.

At their best, our expectations help us to focus on what we are doing. Since expectations remove the doubt from our thoughts they allow us to act in ways that assume that things will work out as we have planned. There's no contract with the Universe that it's actually going to happen. It just allows us to work for what we want without the debilitating influence of doubt.

As we discussed in Chapter 3, doubt is like a fungus that eats away at the structure of our psyche. It undermines our self-confidence and saps our strength and will. It clouds our thinking and disrupts our health and well-being. It is one of those things that keeps us from reaching home. We want to live without doubt, and that's what expectation can do. But there are limits to the power of expectation.

When we start expecting things from other people, we bump up against an even stronger force—free will. If I expect anything from anyone, I am trying to control them. I want them to do what I want. Even if they have agreed to do it, they still have the free will to change their minds and do something entirely different. And that's their right.

So if another person chooses not to do what we expected them to do, we generally get upset. So there we are, having created an expectation, and then feeling unhappy when that expectation is not met.

First of all, it's clear that the feeling we are experiencing is the result of something *we* did. We created the expectation. Sure, the other person was a player in this scenario, but they were just doing whatever it is that they do. We don't control them. We don't really control anyone. What we did was decide how we wanted them to act. Maybe we told them about our expectation, or maybe not. But their actions are wholly independent of our expectation.

Second, the *reaction* we have to whatever it is that they did or didn't do is entirely of our choosing. It may seem that being angry and being disappointed is only natural, but that is just one of many choices we might make. We can decide to ignore them, forgive them quickly, laugh it off, or recognize that they were only doing things in alignment with who they are.

The choice that we make in the way we choose to respond can be informed by how we feel about each option. If we want to be compassionate to ourselves, it is important to make a choice that keeps us feeling as good as possible most of the time. Allowing ourselves to get angry is probably the least pleasurable option we have.

Choosing, usually unconsciously, to be angry when someone else doesn't live up to our expectations is the root of most of the anger people hold. Part of this anger seems to be the shock that what we thought was a definite thing was not so sure after all. It is like a broken contract with reality. And then there is the fact that we didn't get what we wanted. Like a small child, we feel robbed and cheated. We pout and stomp our feet, and, perhaps, cry out loud. When we look at unfulfilled expectations in these terms, the expectations look pretty silly and our reactions even more so.

When we get angry, if we can remember to look behind the situation and see *why* we are getting angry, we typically can do something very quickly to resolve that anger. Usually what we see behind that situation is someone doing something that they thought made sense, but it went against the expectation that we created. Since we are the ones who create these expectations that others seem to ignore, we are responsible for the annoyed feelings we are experiencing. The other person has very little to do with those feelings. They did their thing, and we chose not to like it. If we can realize that the mistake was in creating the expectation in the first place, all the reasons for getting angry disappear. It's like going back in time before the problem and fixing things before they become difficult. No raging, no forgiveness, no heartfelt sharing is required. It is simply an awareness that *we* did something that didn't work.

To treat ourselves kindly and with compassion, we need to be aware of our own responsibility in what we experience. That kindness includes making choices that keep us feeling good as much as possible.

We all know what disappointment feels like, and it isn't good. It's kind of a combination of confusion, betrayal, and anger. Something in the world was supposed to be different than it turned out to be and we don't like it. Often, we look around to see who's to blame. Somebody has not done his or her job properly, and we are suffering because of it.

Disappointment is a severe and harsh emotion. It can instantly fill our entire being and dominate our feelings for very long periods of time. One can think of mothers and fathers whose disappointment in their children lasts all the way up to the parents' deaths. Love affairs that move out of harmony can engender great disappointments, even to the point of life-long grief. Politicians encounter acute disappointment in some of their constituents no matter what these politicians do.

But significant feelings of disappointment can arise with trivial events as well. A hardware store that is out of the tool you need, just missing the bus, or someone not answering your phone call can all be sources of feeling disappointment that may color the rest of the day. And these feelings seem to come out of nowhere, incredibly fast. One minute you're on top of the world, and the next minute your world has just fallen out from beneath you. What happened?

To start with, let's look at disappointment from a broader perspective. We all create versions of the world so that we can fit all the bazillion pieces of life together in a way that makes some sense. Without using tools like meaning and logic, we would be disoriented and confused all the time. Life would be a random series of experiences that had no relationship to one another, and we would have no sense of our place in all of this. So by finding a way to connect events, we build a model in our minds of how the world "works." Whether you call it "the natural order of things" or "just how things happen," these models become our rules of reality.

So, as we build our sense of order in our lives, we naturally incorporate our expectations into our life view. Our expectations become integrated into the fabric of our personal world order. We expect the road to continue on the other side of the hill. We expect the food we buy at the store to be safe. We expect the laws of physics to be immutable. It is so easy to forget that these expectations, concepts of the arrangement of things and events, are our own creations. We have decided that this is how things are or ought to be. Perhaps these ideas are based on patterns we have seen, but they may just as easily be taken from our desires and the imagined fulfillment of those desires.

So, when we find that our expectations or our desires aren't fulfilled to our liking, we may feel disappointed. However, every aspect of this feeling is of our own choosing. We chose to expect something. A desire arose, and we decided to hold onto that desire. And even more importantly, we chose how we reacted to the unfulfilled expectation or desire. We are entirely responsible for how we respond to anything. And the feeling of disappointment that feels so bad is the result of *our choice* to dislike what we are now experiencing!

Rather than saying that our mental understanding of the universe is flawed, we blame someone else for their negligence or stupidity. We might feel angry or hurt or any number of feelings, but they all originate with our decision not to like what we are encountering. But what we often overlook is that *we* have brought these feelings on ourselves. And that can change!

This is the soft underbelly of disappointment, the vulnerable spot on this terrible dragon. We have done it to ourselves. And we can do things differently if we want to have a different emotional experience. If we like, we can choose to view life from an adventurer's perspective and say that we don't really know what happens next, that our sense of the order of things is only a working theory, and that the unexpected is what is significant to our growth and expansion. We can dissolve our disappointment instantly by changing how we react to unpredicted events.

We can choose to be delighted at the surprise or the new opportunity to explore something different. If it's comfort or love we were expecting, we might use that moment to find those things within ourselves. If it's mechanical things that don't work the way we expected, we can use that moment to relax and enjoy the pleasures of the things that do work. If it is something that someone has done that was not what we wanted, we can admire the miracle of free will and enjoy what this person has decided to present to us. Every instance of disappointment is an opportunity to reorder our world to one that brings us more joy, not less. It is our choice!

Two everyday fears that we might be tempted to take on are the fear of doing something where we might be disappointed, and the fear of disappointing others. The first one, the fear of a choice we make leading to our own disappointment, is based on the idea that disappointment is the inevitable result of a failed expectation. This notion is responsible for a great deal of unnecessary misery. As we've seen, disappointment is a choice. So, being afraid of being disappointed is being afraid that we might choose to not like something. It's a pretty silly thing to be afraid of our own choices.

The other fear, being afraid of disappointing others, is based on the same idea: that a failed expectation unavoidably leads to disappointment. In this case, it is to be concerned that someone else will choose to create an expectation and then choose to be disappointed. This is an attempt to take responsibility for that other person's feelings.

Most of the time when we want to help others, we want to help them regain their personal power. Powerless people tend to be very unhappy. And if we have a desire to see them happier, helping them to restore their power is an important step. But taking away someone else's power to make choices for themselves is counterproductive. So, protecting someone else from their own choices does not serve them well. If they choose to create expectations and then choose to be disappointed, we can compassionately point out to them—if they seem open to it—how expectations and disappointment work. But to protect them from themselves heads down a path of powerlessness that is unhealthy for all concerned.

When I encounter people who honestly find that they are afraid of disappointing people, and there are many who are afraid, I offer them an exercise to help let go of that fear. It's a little facetious, but it works, and it only takes a week. The exercise is to intentionally disappoint at least three people a day for seven days. They are allowed to disappoint one person three times each day, if they want to.

The point here isn't to create more disappointment in the world. It's to help people get over the fear that if someone else blames you for disappointing them, you won't be liked, respected, loved, or whatever else matters most to you. We are not responsible for other people's disappointment. To be disappointed is their choice; and putting the responsibility on you is dishonest and hurtful.

Another aspect in this exercise is noticing how crippling the fear of disappointing others is. So many people restrain and inhibit themselves out of fear of being blamed for disappointing someone else. To be fair to those with this fear, disappointment is often used as a tool of manipulation and has probably been used on them. All of us have probably been admonished at some point with, "Now, don't disappoint me!" This is a cruel misuse of responsibility and a form of emotional abuse.

When we live with the fear that we may be blamed for someone else's disappointment, we have internalized this abuse. To be compassionate towards ourselves and to reclaim the power to come home we need to stop abusing ourselves regarding disappointment.

Kindness toward others would lead us to not want to see others hurt. And when others don't like something we've done, it seems natural to feel responsible to some degree for their feelings. But we need to remember that we are not in charge of their lives. We do what is necessary in our own lives, taking into account those around us. But kindness to ourselves needs to come first. Without that we can never be at home in ourselves, and it is only there that we can genuinely help others, if we choose to.

We develop healthier attitudes of self-confidence and self-love when we honor people's right to run their own lives. That includes us. Assisting with love and compassion while resisting the temptation to take care of another's feelings is the empowered way of caring.

Not all angers are the result of unfulfilled expectations. Sometimes we encounter experiences that are both unpleasant and not obviously of our own making. Somebody robs us on the street, we drive over a pothole and ruin a tire, or we miss a plane flight because of a delay getting to the airport, for example. We can certainly find someone or something to blame. But if we are to find a pleasure strategy that maximizes our overall pleasure, blaming someone or something won't do much for us.

It is at times like these when it behooves us to remember what our objectives are. We can choose the road of anger, and that will give us a small sense of power in a powerless situation. That does indeed make us feel a little better. But there are other, more powerful, choices we can make. By letting go of the anger or blame and turning our attention to the things that are truly important to us, we can stay emotionally level and achieve our larger goal—to be happy. This doesn't mean we think that it is okay when we are experiencing any of these things. It means that they are sufficiently trivial to not get in our way.

Being kind to ourselves means taking care of the inner "child" in us who didn't get his or her way. That part of us often needs to be reminded of what we want most and what we must do to attain it.

Three Powerful Ways to Use Expectations

First, expect that whatever happens, you will be just fine. That is, the Universe will be looking out for you in ways that you may not understand. Understood or not, expect that unseen forces are working in your favor. This is using the tool of trust carefully. You may not get exactly what you were hoping for, but most likely you will get something that works well for you in other ways.

Second, expect that your experiences will be to your liking. When you're anticipating any event, either something you're looking forward to or just the opposite, by expecting that you will like and enjoy the experience, you most likely will. In general, we get what we expect to get. So why not expect the best, always? Say "yes" to the finest you can imagine and expect it. Just remember that the expectations we have of other people don't work very well, but expectations of events and experiences do.

And third, expect that the primary organization of your life, whether you call it your purpose, calling, or plan is unfolding the way it needs to and that it is good. In general, things go much more smoothly when we relax and with much more difficulty when we get tense and worry. The phrase "let go and let God" makes this very point.

If an expectation isn't fulfilled, the first thing to remember is that we created the expectation to begin with. Taking responsibility for our expectations means that we have no one to blame. All too often we create expectations within a limited perspective. We may have used the tool of expectation to focus our energies, but we didn't realize all the factors at hand. If, for reasons unknown to us, we didn't get the results we were looking for, there may well be lots of other issues involved that we either don't know about or have ignored. It's no one's fault, and it's not the end of the world.

For instance, let's say we didn't get promoted to the position in our current employment that we wanted and expected. It may be that it's not yet our time for that position and it was the right time for the person who got the job. It may be that we sabotaged our energies with conflicting desires, say a desire actually to change professions. It may be that decisions we made earlier in our career with this company have had a substantial effect on our present situation. Expectations are only tools. They work well when used correctly, but like any useful tool, they have their limitations.

Second, we want to look at the unfulfilled expectation in as broad a perspective as we can. There are likely one or more very positive things that are the result of that different reality. Paying more attention to what has worked out in our favor than what did not is a way of harvesting this experience and utilizing what has been presented to us. The art to using expectations positively is to use these instruments when they work and to let them go when they don't.

So, how do we make a conscious, effective expectation? Well, it's more than just saying the words, "I expect this to happen." It is a determined choice not to let doubt creep in. Once we've decided to use the tool of expectation we have to make sure it stays operational. That is, when doubts arise, and they probably will, we need to dismiss them and not allow them to gain a foothold in our thoughts. It requires a certain amount of resolve to resist the siren's call of doubt. Once again, our trust is there to be used instead of doubt. Remember, logic can work for anything. We can always come up with reasons to do any particular action, so being swayed by logic isn't a sign of wisdom. Trust, perhaps more appropriately called faith in this case, says, "Now that I've made my choice of action, I will follow it through."

The trick to this is to expect without being too attached to the particulars. We might expect to have a good time at a party, but we want to stay flexible regarding what fun things might happen. We might expect to be successful in a new business, but we need to allow success to come in unexpected ways. We might expect to have a healthy loving relationship, but we need to be aware that things change and our ideas about what a healthy loving relationship is may need to change as well.

The point is that an expectation is just a device that we can use to aim our energies. If we accept that there will likely be some differences between our vision and what we encounter, we can be adaptable to whatever happens without getting upset.

Expectations are like apples. We know what apples taste like, in general, and we know what this one will likely taste like; but each apple tastes slightly different. Some are better than others. But, if we usually like apples, we will probably like this one. We expect to like it. But we have enough experience to know that we may not, and that's okay. The art of expectation is to hold it loosely so as not to be pulled off center should the expectation go awry.

To treat ourselves with the compassion and the kindness we deserve, we need to use expectations wisely. Expectations are marvelous tools when used to help us stay focused on what we want and what we are doing. By using their trait of doubtlessness we can maneuver without being distracted by our imagined fears. If something is expected to happen but doesn't, we can take responsibility for that expectation and look instead for whatever was positive in the situation.

Meditation 6
Putting Childhood to Rest

I remember having lots of toys and lots of time to play with them when I was little. I remember rain, and wind, and cold, and hot. I remember going on great adventures. I remember lots of things about being a child. Some of those things were wonderful, and some of them were not. But they are memories now, and I am a different person today.

I remember being fed and cared for. I remember wearing clothes that didn't fit for very long. I remember learning how to take care of my body's needs. I remember that someone helped me when I got sick and tried to help me feel better. Sometimes I got the love I wanted, and sometimes I didn't.

So many people helped me when I was little. I don't remember most of their names, but I'm grateful for all the help I got as a child. I know that most of the people closest to me tried hard to make things good for me. And I'm thankful for them.

There were some things in my childhood that I really didn't like. Some people didn't treat me the way I wanted them to. But that's over now, and I have learned to enjoy today.

It's Time to Come Home

Sometimes I have memories of things that frighten me. When those memories come, I can also remember that I am safe now and there's nothing to be afraid of now. I feel the fear and then reassure myself that it's all over and I am safe now.

As I look back now, it seems that people should have taken better care of me. Sometimes I feel a little angry that they didn't do what I think they should have done. If they had done their job better, perhaps I wouldn't feel the way I do now.

But, maybe it's just possible that they did the best they knew how to do. Perhaps they had their own difficulties to deal with. And maybe they didn't have the perspective I have now about how things might have been done back then.

I don't have to carry this anger about what other people did and didn't do around with me. I want to be happy, and this anger doesn't make me happy. I think I will turn my focus to the things that make me happy and let the other things float away.

I don't have to excuse people for what they have done, but I also don't have to keep hurting myself with these thoughts. I put these old thoughts away now and turn my focus to the things that bring me joy.

I don't have to totally forget my unpleasant memories, but I think I will put them away now, like out of season clothes in some old trunk. Sometime I will forgive all those people who didn't do what I wanted them to do, but I don't have to do that today.

When I go to sleep, I will make sure I don't forget the memories of wonderful things that happened when I was a child. I want to keep those little treasures. When I think of them, they delight me, and I want lots of that in my life.

What is past is gone now. Today was such a rich day with lots of things to experience and feel. I give thanks for the beauty of this day. I give thanks for the friends and loved ones in my life. I give thanks for all the joy in my life. And I look forward to more joy tomorrow.

Just trust yourself, then you will know how to live.
Johann Wolfgang von Goethe

*Simple kindness to one's self and to all that lives
is the most transformational force of all.*
David Hawkins

Chapter 7

The Past Needs Kindness, Too

One of the consequences of looking at a space-time continuum is the perspective that there is a past that has "caused" the present, and what we do in the present "causes" the future. Thus, if what we experience is not to our liking, either we have done something wrong, or some outside force has interfered with our plans and "caused" this undesired experience. Regarding the part of this experience that we are responsible for, if we have made a mistake the unpleasant experience is our punishment for that mistake.

This idea is also predicated on the notion that there is some place or state of being that we are trying to achieve. If we are attempting to have a loving and harmonious monogamous marriage and we succumb to the temptation to have sex with someone else, we will probably frame the situation as a mistake afterward. There is an idea that if we want to get a specific result, we need to make as few mistakes as possible to get there.

However, there is another way of looking at things. If we view our lives from the perspective that this moment is all there is, each moment is filled with hundreds of choices that take us to the next moment. We can't see beyond this next moment, but we can choose on the basis of all our wisdom, desires, loves, and inspiration. Thus, each moment is a step along a marvelous adventure: an adventure with some vague headings and with unknowns at every turn. We change the idea of mistakes into a notion of useful experiments that have shown us things we don't want.

From the perspective of looking back on some of those choices, we can see that other choices *might* have worked out in ways that we would have preferred. But how were we to know how things would work out? Sometimes we can say, "Well, I should have seen the consequences more clearly." (Actual language would probably be more like, "Damn! *That* was dumb!") For some reason, we seem to believe that we're supposed to know and understand everything. It's as though we're told, "It's all in the book," referring to some rulebook, written or not.

I'm here to say, "No, it's not!" What's often in the rulebook is what someone else thinks is the best way to live, based on his or her own wisdom, experience, and the inner guidance for their own life.

In each moment, we draw upon whatever we can to help us make the choices that take us to the next moment. We have no choice but to experiment, going down one path then another as in a labyrinth, until we either get to someplace we like, or we go back and try a different way. We can't see over the labyrinth hedge; we can only learn bit by bit what works and what doesn't work. A choice that seems to go somewhere is intrinsically no better than an alternative that doesn't. Both kinds of decisions are essential to our learning.

Once we give up on the notion that we are *supposed* to be getting somewhere, we become empowered to focus on what is happening at this moment. As it happens, this is precisely where things like joy, love, happiness, pleasure, harmony, and contentment live. How ironic it is that all of our efforts to complete the *essential* tasks in life, and focusing on their future completion, are about getting to this place of presence—when merely focusing on the present does it instantly.

So from the perspective of an adventurer, there are no mistakes, only choices that one doesn't want to make again. From the standpoint of loving ourselves, understanding the results of our decisions brings us wisdom, not some shaming of ourselves. I like to say that I never make mistakes. Sometimes I do things that don't work out nearly as well as I'd like or require some damage control. But each experience makes me a wiser person, a person more capable of choosing pleasure in the next moment.

It makes no sense to criticize ourselves for making choices that don't work out. As already pointed out, we made the best decision we knew how to make. But making ourselves feel bad for making that choice compounds the difficulty. And as we've seen, criticism not only doesn't work, it makes things worse.

Regret, and saying to ourselves that something shouldn't have happened the way it did, is a way of fighting with who we are. This battle usually involves some guilt or shame and a deep wound to our self-esteem, which feels awful.

The logic behind this goes something like, "I wish I could have done things differently. My life is damaged because of this." This statement is, of course, a belief, and a common one at that. But it is a belief that is highly self-destructive. We are telling ourselves 1) that in some way we are responsible for something happening, or not happening, that has a significant adverse impact on our lives, and 2) that it is irreversible.

One of the things that we can easily overlook is the relationship between memory and imagination. If you think they are separate things, I invite you to look inside and see if you can find the dividing line between them. I think you'll have a tough time finding that line. In fact, keep looking; I think you'll see that your memory is just one aspect of imagination. You don't remember everything that happened in any given situation or event; you remember what you said the last time you thought about it or told the story to someone. You fill in the details with your imagination. That's why memories are remarkably unreliable and change noticeably over time. We will talk about the stories you tell later in this book. But for now, be mindful that your regret is based on shaky ground.

Something else to pay attention to is whether or not you believe that you should be perfect, or something similar. If you feel that you should have known better, about whatever, then you are butting your head against the wall of learning. If you were supposed to know it all, you wouldn't have to learn anything and you should be perfectly happy now. However, if you are living your life as a human being, learning is a constant and ongoing aspect of life. When you come across something that didn't work the way you thought it should, or you did what you later figured out was not good, you learned something. Perhaps it was a lesson that needed repeating and further learning was necessary.

Rather than regretting something and feeling bad about yourself for doing or not doing it, there are many ways of treating yourself with compassion instead. The first thing, though, is to deal with the belief that things shouldn't have gone the way they did. That is a denial of your reality. Accepting what happened and recognizing that it is something that is now out of the present moment and out of reach to immediately alter allows you the space to change some aspects of your experience. As in anything that you want to change in your life, accepting what is currently in front of you is the first step. Changing how you look at that experience, then, is the next step.

In this culture, it is a virtue to remember as much as we can and forget as little as possible. We have systems to help us increase our memories, programs to follow, abundant theories to consider, and condolences and jokes when our memories are not what we think they should be. However, this point of view overlooks the crucial role that forgetting plays, not only in everyday life but also in how we craft lives of joy and pleasure.

We remember things according to their emotional apparel. Naked thoughts are hard to remember, but thoughts with brightly colored accessories come back to us quickly. If we try to remember the particulars of a party, for instance, we rarely remember the details in chronological order. We think of the things that had the most emotional impact on us first. Then we remember other details in descending order of flashiness or impact.

Events and experiences that were unpleasant in some fashion are remembered the same way. The ones that have the most visceral content are the ones we remember most easily.

But not all memories are useful to us. For example, if I remember how you treated me some years ago, I may continue to feel resentment towards you. That resentment will probably (1) not feel good in the present moment, (2) prevent me from having any kind of loving connection with you, (3) influence my relations with others, and (4) affect my ability to enjoy what I'm doing now. Hanging on to that memory poisons me.

Another example might be about mistakes I think I've made in my life. If I spend time remembering the things that I have done that didn't work out as I would have liked them to!, I may well start sliding down into depression. That kind of feeling is utterly useless to me. And if I let myself focus on the memories of my personal disappointments, I can get deeply despondent.

An additional example might be the memory of the lover who, after pledging undying love, left with my best friend. The feelings associated with that kind of memory are so toxic that there ought to be mandatory warning signs.

There is no need or utility in remembering most of these resentments, disappointments, betrayals, mistakes, losses, missed opportunities, or broken dreams. If we are serious about choosing to be happy and being kind to ourselves, we need to be aware of the choices we make in each moment. And, optimally, we make decisions that increase our level of pleasure at that time. Memories of the unpleasant things do just the opposite; they only increase the level of misery in our lives.

You may be questioning the wisdom of intentionally forgetting "important" events in your life, even if they were unpleasant. Perhaps there are some things that you might want to remember in order to tell a story of your triumph over adversity. Or maybe there is some valuable lesson that needs reinforcement. But for the most part, these memories only keep us out of our joy.

So, how do we let go of these memories?

To answer this question, let's first look at the nature of importance. Things are important to us because we have strong feelings about them or because of them. My parents are important to me because my feelings of love for them are robust and deep. My career is important to me because I feel passionate about the work I do. My garden is important to me because of the enormous joy I get just walking through it. Memories are important to us because of the feelings involved with them. Strong feelings lead to increased importance. If my feelings of jealousy regarding my errant lover are powerful, that situation is crucial to me. But importance works like a radio. Not only do we need to tune into the situation, but we also have a volume control. We can turn down the level of importance.

The easiest way to turn down importance is to change our focus. That might be sliding the dial a little off the situation, as in thinking of other things. Or we can change our relative perspective, by simply moving the volume dial lower just a little. In the case of the runaway lover, I might pull back from my intense focus on the hurt she has "caused" me and recognize that it's silly to think that there is only one person who can love me the way I want to be loved. There must be hundreds of wonderful candidates for that job. The importance of that abandonment is diminished each time I pull back a little further and see things from a broader perspective. There are lots more important things for me to be putting my attention on. If I don't start feeling better fairly quickly I can realize that the issue isn't about her at all, it's about my own level of self-esteem. That's a very different issue.

So, when we want to let go of a memory, the way to most efficiently do so is to take away the emotional content of that issue: we reduce or remove its importance. Once a memory is no longer remarkable, it fades behind things that are important.

It's Time to Come Home

This kind of forgetting does not erase memory,
it lays the emotion surrounding the memory to rest.
Clarissa Pinkola Estes

For centuries, Hawaiians have had a marvelous conflict resolution system in their culture called *ho'oponopono*. In it, every member of the community gets a chance to express their observation of a problem, their own part in the problem, and what they think is needed to bring the issue to resolution. After it has been decided what will resolve the issue, anyone who cannot forgive another is banished by the community until they can forgive. When anger and resentment are allowed to linger, the community is unable to prosper and be happy. Another aspect of this is that each person is forbidden to ever to bring this issue up again. That is, everyone is expected to forget about it entirely. This allows everyone to get back into a loving connection with one another without lingering resentments. This would be a valuable practice in our world today.

Forgetting, even forgetting the things we have enjoyed, is a critical part of crafting a magnificent life. When everything is fresh and new, we see its beauty more clearly. When judgments, good or bad, do not cloud our minds, we discover the people and things that we surround ourselves with anew. Life is an even greater adventure to those who know how to forget and learn in new ways.

Our sense of worth, of well-being, even our sanity depends upon our remembering.
But, alas, our sense of worth, our well-being, our sanity
also depend upon our forgetting.
Joyce Appleby

The impulse to consider the "what-ifs?" in life is a natural one, borne of a desire to stay as safe as possible and avoid hidden dangers. On the face of it, it seems like an essential part of self-care and self-preservation. We want to consider all the probabilities in our future so that we can make the wisest choices.

The problem comes when we only focus on the "what-ifs?" that we don't want. This is, of course, what worry is. But when we focus just on our problems and what might happen that's "bad," we overlook two critical things.

The first thing we overlook is that things working out in our favor are at least as likely to happen as things going the other way. Not paying attention to the good outcomes means that we often miss them when they are in front of us. The "what-if?" events which are much better than we could ever have imagined need to be taken into account just as much as any other possibilities. To neglect these prospects is to close the door to significant contributions to our joy.

The other thing that we ignore is that we think better and see more when we are relaxed, and thus we can make better choices. If instead of worrying we *decide* to trust that whatever outcome appears will be beneficial, we can let go of toxic worrying and enjoy life.

And we don't do ourselves any favors when we continually focus on our problems. Challenges are a natural part of life and when we find one, facing it quickly and doing something about it is usually the wisest course of action. However, when we are continually trying to fix problems we often lose sight of why we are trying to fix the problems in the first place. We fix problems so that we can get back to enjoying our lives. But when we seek out problems to fix, as in doing our "shadow" work or doing lots of self-help workshops, we stay in the vibration of needing to be fixed.

It's a cliché, but a useful one, that when a woman just wants someone to listen to her, the man wants to fix the problem. It's as though the man (or woman) is afraid of the intimacy of simply feeling, particularly when feeling a lower vibration. The same kind of situation becomes a habit when we continually look for ways to fix our problems but shy away from spending prolonged time enjoying what's in front of us.

I'm as guilty of this as anyone. I step into my kitchen, and the first thing I notice is whatever dirty dishes there might be. I don't stop to enjoy how cool my kitchen is, and both its beauty and its sweet functionality. I look for what needs to be done. The same is true with my garden. I can enjoy the beauty and fragrances for a moment, and then I start seeing the weeds that need pulling, the bushes that need trimming, and the fallen branches that need to be picked up.

This habit isn't a terrible problem in my outer world, although it's symptomatic of my inner world. But it's the inner world where this habit of looking to fix things is most pernicious.

If I want to get good at creating the life I want, I need to be very mindful of the thoughts I am holding that then get energized and become my reality. Each of my thoughts affects my experience, and if I want to improve my experience I need to improve my thoughts, particularly the ones I'm not paying much attention to. *All* of my thoughts affect my happiness. So if I am holding on to thoughts that this, that, and the other thing aren't right, this is the vibration with which I am creating my life.

This notion is particularly evident in thoughts about lack. "Oh, I shouldn't buy that one; it's too expensive." "I really want to be able to afford a new apartment." "I just want to find a man/woman to love me." These statements seem innocuous enough, but they come from a belief that these things don't currently exist in our experience. And any focus on these thoughts only strengthens them.

So the obvious thing is to not focus on our lack, but instead on our already existing abundance. But that's not always so easy. It is mostly a function of our belief that if we get all of our problems fixed, we'll be golden.

In a mechanistic world, that is the way things work. We fix our car, and it runs well. We fix our medical problems, and then we get to go out dancing again. We fix our tax problems, and we get to stay out of jail.

But that's not how the energetic world works. The issues of the outer world are only the products of our inner world. So fixing the external world problems does nothing for our inner world problems.

Our inner world problems arise from how we are looking at our experience. If we look at what's going on as a problem, then it becomes a problem. If, however, we look at the very same thing as a neutral or, even better, as a positive experience with things to learn and grow by, we create our outer world very differently.

One way to do this is to inwardly say "thank you" for everything that comes our way. Another way is to constantly remind ourselves that "everything is working out perfectly." Another way is to get into the habit of looking for the pleasure in everything, seeking out what can be enjoyed. Each of these approaches keeps our vibration high, and thus we create better things for ourselves without having to focus so hard on getting our desires met.

I would never suggest that we overlook the things that are hurting us or have the potential to do so. We need to take care of ourselves. But the most important thing is to stay in as high a vibration as possible. If I want to enjoy my life, then I continually need to practice—practice enjoying myself.

Resetting the Past

I don't think that many of us notice the very moment when we go from accepting that one pleasure is finished and we are now ready for the next one. But I find that moment to be very interesting. We come to a place where we are no longer satisfied with what is. The pleasure may have dissipated so much that it no longer feels particularly good, or we may see an even greater pleasure around the corner, or perhaps we are simply ready for something different. In any case, there is a subtle shift in us. Something inside has pushed us to move on, perhaps reluctantly.

With so many opportunities available, recognized or not, these are the little moments when the choices we have made and the rules we have created about what is possible and what is not come into play. How we are crafting our lives reveals itself here. In each of these special moments we reset ourselves, we change the direction of our lives a little. I believe that at these moments we are trying to get a little closer to fulfilling some deeper desire, one that has probably never been voiced but which has been calling us for a long time. We get closer every time we go from unsatisfactoriness to something that looks to be more pleasurable. Each time we try to make our lives a little better, each time we pay attention to what we want, we learn a little bit more about ourselves and bring ourselves into alignment with our core being just a little bit more. It is these moments when we can most easily hear our calls to wholeness.

One of the key pieces to letting go of some pleasure is to admit that those marvelous experiences that we enjoyed so much are over. When we are feeling sad or, more deeply, feeling grief, we are feeling a kind of anger that things have changed when we didn't want them to. Sometimes we feel that we have been robbed in some way, that there has been a great injustice done, that this just isn't right. However, the longer we hold on to that anger, the longer we get to feel the effects of it. These effects are familiar to all of us: tiredness, mild to severe depression, pessimism, etc.

Acknowledging that things have changed is a gift we give to ourselves. It is an act of kindness that soothes our soul even while it opens the door to uncertainty. We know the truth of it but find that truth unpalatable. This is one of those special times when we need to take care of ourselves as we would a sick child. The more tender we can be, the more gentle, caring, and loving, the more effective we will be in the long run. Not only are we acknowledging that things have changed, but that we have changed as well. The parts of our world that we have cherished are different now. We have come to know a part within us that we love (even though the object of our love may be someone or something outside of us.) Even if we remember that we will always be able to cherish this person or thing, it seems as though we've lost a part of who we are. It may take a certain amount of courage to face ourselves in the light of these changes. But we can do it.

Acknowledging the changes is the magical key that opens other doors to joy. Without that key we are locking ourselves out of our rightful happiness.

So how do we put all of this together and let go of pleasures that have come to an end? I recommend a three-step process: gratitude, acknowledgment of change, and refocusing our thoughts on new pleasures. This is the time to invoke the magic of gratitude thoroughly, taking as much time as we need to in order to feel it fully. Then, when we feel ready, we say, preferably out loud, that we acknowledge that things have changed. The effect is more powerful when we can physically hear ourselves say what is in our mind.

A sample statement might look like this:

I give thanks for all the joy I had with (whoever or whatever we are letting go of). But I recognize that things have changed. I turn my focus now towards all the new joys ahead of me.

Gratitude and acknowledgment that things have changed leave us in a place that is perfect for looking forward to the next opportunity for pleasure. By giving ourselves closure on one chapter we are ready to open a new one. This is the process of resetting ourselves, and it is basically a change of focus. When we have that emotional sense of the completion of the last experience, we can look around us, savor what we are experiencing in the present moment and then move on. We can move back into our adventurer mode to see what else lies out there to discover.

There is nothing wrong with leaving the past behind. It was great (or not), but it's not today. We don't owe the past anything. It is life already lived. Now is the time for new life. If we hold our focus well, we can be confident that the joys to come will be even better than the ones we have experienced so far. Resetting ourselves means relaxing into the openness of infinite possibilities. At some level we are initiating a new adventure. Remembering the pleasures of adventure and joys of new connections helps us to walk away from the past with confidence and hope.

So the question becomes, if you could change things in your past, would you be happier today? Probably not. Because the happiness you experience now is dependent on the choices you are making *today*! It is the things that you focus on, the things you appreciate or complain about, that constitute your happiness. Let the things of yesterday go; enjoy the pleasures of today, and create even more joy for yourself and others tomorrow.

You are not today what you were yesterday. And tomorrow you certainly don't have to be what you have been today. You are in charge of what aspects of your past you will make important. You can make whatever choices you want about how the past will affect you. Essentially, you are creating your past in the present. Choose wisely, dear one.

Meditation 7

It Is Safe To Be Who I Am

The dog lies on its pillow and curls its tail comfortably. The birds and squirrels are going about their business. The trees are content to be trees. The sun is just happy to be. And it's safe for me to be who I am.

Today I will do what I can. I do what I'm able to do, and I let the rest go. I don't have to be more than I am. I only need to be me.

I am having lots of experiences today. Some are fun, some not so much. But they are all my *experiences.* I *have those experiences, and now they become a part of me. They are* all *okay, and so am I.*

There may be things that I would have liked to do that I won't do today. Perhaps there are things that I would have liked to have done differently. But I do my best in each moment, and I learn a few things along the way. And it's okay for me to be who I am.

I look out at the world, and I see many things. I see the world through my own eyes and look at the world from my *point of view. I have a unique perspective, and it's okay for me to see the world through my eyes.*

I have so many thoughts each day. Some I like better than others. But they are my thoughts, and they're all fine. I get to think whatever thoughts I want. It's safe for me to think whatever thoughts I want. It's safe to be who I am.

And I have a lot of feelings each day. So many feelings, it's hard to notice them all. I like some of my feelings, and I don't care for others. But they are all my *feelings, and it's safe for me to feel what I feel.*

It's Time to Come Home

I am breathing today so I know I'm alive. I like breathing, and I like being alive. What a strange experience it is to be alive, to be an individual walking on this Earth. I give thanks for this life. I give thanks for all the parts of this complex life of mine. I give thanks for me.

I take a quiet moment now before I go on. I don't have to do anything just now. My body likes this. My legs get to rest. My arms get to rest. My head gets to rest. My belly gets to rest. My back gets to rest. My bones get to rest. Even my skin gets to rest. My whole body gets to rest for right now.

My mind gets to rest now, too. I don't have to solve any problems right now. I don't have to remember what I have to do today. I can simply enjoy the peace I am experiencing right now. This peace feels good. This peace feels very good to me.

I'm grateful for all the beauty in my life, the things and animals around me, the world I live in, and especially the people in my life. I am grateful for my life, my own unique life, that's not exactly like anyone else's. It's safe to be me. And I like that.

It's safe to be who I am.

Do not be satisfied with the stories that come before you.
Unfold your own myth.
Rumi

Chapter 8

The Stories that Make Us: Talking to Ourselves

Have you ever noticed how the way you tell a story changes how you feel? For instance, when you ask how I'm doing and I tell you that I'm okay, I also hear that I'm okay, and that's that. But if I tell you that I'm doing great, I can feel myself moving into a more robust kind of experience. And the same is true if I say to you that I'm feeling poorly, sad, down, depressed, tired, or miserable. When I then add a story to explain how I feel, that description then becomes my reality. Our stories, the way we describe our lives and explain who we are, actively create our reality and our experiences of life.

Here's a little story about stories.
I was walking down the street the other day, and I encountered a distraught young woman. Feeling compassionate, I stopped to see if I could do anything for her. She told me, between fits of crying and screaming, that her boyfriend of several years was trying to break up with her. I asked her how she knew that was what he was doing. She said that she had seen him talking to a pretty woman in an office a short while ago, and then he had come out smiling broadly. She was sure that he was more interested in this pretty woman than he was in her. I suggested that he might have been trying to get a better paying job so that he could marry her and support her in her life. She

immediately brightened up and began smiling. Her whole vibration shifted, and she became quite radiant.

But then she said that he was always looking at pretty girls, and this was probably just another example of him chasing someone else. She then started to cry again. I offered the suggestion that perhaps he loved beauty in general and the beauty of women in particular, and that that was why he had chosen *her* to be his girlfriend. Again she brightened up, pulled her shoulders back, and clearly felt good about herself once more.

The renewed brightness started to fade as she said to me, "You're probably right, but I'm not sure I'm good enough for him." While I was thinking about how I was going to respond to her, she was stewing in this self-doubt and she simply darkened and hunched over again. It was as if someone had abruptly turned down her inner lights.

I offered the thought that *he* must have thought she was good enough since he had gone out with her for so long. And besides, trying to live up to some notion of perfection or "good enough" was like telling a rose to smell differently. We all are who we are, and that's all we need to be.

She thought that one over for a bit and seemed to feel a little better. She then stated that he was the only one who could make her happy and that if she lost him, she would be devastated. I reminded her that if he was in charge of her happiness, she might never be happy; but if she chose to be the one in charge of her happiness, she could be happy any time she liked. I then invited her to decide right then and there to be happy.

She looked at me as though I was a cross between an obnoxious drunk and an angel. It was a very curious expression. But, as the thought sank in, she brightened up once again and said that she was determined to be happy and thanked me before going on her way.

She had had six different powerful experiences in just a few minutes, and nothing had happened to her except the stories she told herself.

It is imperative that we understand that it's the story we tell that makes us feel hurt. We define our reality with the story we are telling, whether we are telling it to other people or just to ourselves. Any time we tell a story that makes us feel bad, we are treating ourselves cruelly. And it's completely unnecessary. We can tell our stories in any way we want. We can tell them in ways that make us feel bad, or we can find a way to tell them that make us feel good about ourselves.

We Are Always Telling Ourselves Stories About Our Lives

As human beings, we need to make some sense of our world. We seek to understand how things work so that we can survive and thrive. So we make meanings that connect the numerous and diverse elements of our lives to understand what is going on. But meanings are created; they come from our imagination. Let's take a moment to look at how we do this.

If we have an experience of some kind, Experience A, and then we have another experience, Experience B, we want to find out how they are related. They may not necessarily have any natural relationship, but the urge to find one leads to the creation of meaning. Maybe we say A "caused" B, or vice versa. Or perhaps we assume that they arose together from some unknown source that was good or bad, evil or divine. When we experience something else we then look for the connection to what we "know," and a new meaning is created.

How we create the meaning is our choice. We can find a meaning that makes us feel empowered, or we can find one that makes us victims of some more powerful being. We can create meanings that help us bond with other people, or we can create them to feed our fears about others.

We need meanings. They allow us to navigate in this world and not have to question everything all the time. But we need to remember that we choose what the meaning is. We make it up. These meanings get strung together in stories that then become our realities.

It is helpful to remember from time to time that we have made up the stories that frame our reality, and that the stories that we have been telling for so long may no longer be serving us well. We can take a look at anything and make up several different stories about it, and whichever story we decide to believe in will become our "true" reality. The experience of that reality is then a function of how we have set it up.

And we can reframe any story we have and come up with a different reality based on the very same facts. The choice is ours as to what story we will tell. While our power comes from our choices and our will, the energy behind those choices is our emotional vibration. The higher our vibration, the more effective we can be. *Our power comes from our personal stories.*

Here's a little exercise for you to try. The function of this exercise is to become aware of your stories and to see how they affect how you feel. You can do this with another person, taking a minute or two to answer each of the four questions in turn. Or you can do this on your own and write down your answers. Because this involves doing two things at once, telling your story and monitoring your feelings, it is probably easier to try to think of the answers with some sort of outward communication like writing or speaking.

Pay attention to how you are crafting each story. How does your story affect your feelings and your energy level? To start with, simply assess how you're feeling on a scale of 1 to 10, with 1 being extremely low and 10 being ecstatic. After you tell each story, rate your vibration level again to see if and how it might have changed. Please don't judge your responses or try to clean them up. You can do that later. Right now, just pay attention to your feelings as you tell them.

1. How good were your parents at being parents?

2. Who or what has hurt you, traumatized you, or demoralized you? If nobody currently fits this description, answer about what you used to think.
3. What event or events from your past have defined you the most?
4. Why aren't you happier now than you want to be? What is holding you back in your life?

Did you find that your assessment of how you were feeling changed as you told your stories? Did emotional things come up for you that affected how you felt? Remember, your feelings mostly follow your thoughts. So, as you had thoughts of powerful feelings, those feelings likely asserted themselves. You can see that each time you tell any story about yourself, you are affecting your very being. To be kind to ourselves, we need to pay attention to how we make ourselves feel with our stories.

In many ways, we are the story we're telling ourselves. Most people aren't conscious of their stories. They just tell them as natural facts of life. But we define ourselves by our stories. We say "this is who I am," with our stories. And by doing this, we are recreating ourselves in the present moment according to the blueprint that we just uttered.

As we tell our stories, we emphasize certain parts and ignore other parts. By doing that we make some things more important than others. The elements of our story that we focus on become bigger. That's the easiest place to start changing our stories. Move the emphasis and importance around.

The best stories we can tell are about love. No matter how tragic we think our story may be, we can always find some way of either learning more about love or opening into new arenas of love. It's important to include what we have gone through in the stories, and to include what we have harvested in the way of useful lessons. Every hardship, for instance, has lessons of compassion. Now we understand better how other people feel and what they may have gone through. We can find more profound levels of our being as a result of having these powerful experiences. But we need to take the time to see what we've gained to finally put these stories to rest.

Ultimately, we are the only source of our stories. They are our responsibility. We put things together to help us understand our experiences. This takes place in our minds according to our unique filters and assumptions. They are our own creation and, as such, it is important to craft them carefully. We want to make the most out of how we are putting our lives together with these stories.

But, naturally, we want to be true to ourselves and not avoid things that may hurt us later. We want to make sure that what we say is true. But truth is disturbingly flexible. Something that we regard as true one day may change for us the next day with new information or perspectives. The truest stories, though, are the ones that work for us. We judge our stories by how well they seem to account for what we have experienced and also how satisfied we feel with those explanations. The trick here is to look for explanations that make us feel that we've been honest with ourselves and yet make us feel as positive and self-loving as possible. We'll work with this more shortly.

So we want to choose stories that make us feel competent, aware, and powerful in the sense of having considerable influence on our environment. I find that changing our personal stories is the most effective way to accomplish long-term healing. It is incredible, to me, how quickly a life can change with little changes to a person's life story.

Shamans were the original storytellers. They told stories of creation, why things happened, and who to talk to about changing things. But their primary function was to aid in healing. And a big part of any healing is changing the narrative. That's why placebos work so often. If we believe that something is changing or has changed, our reality tends to reflect that. This works both ways, of course. If we believe that something awful has happened to us, we tend to make that our "truth." That's how curses work. If we ignore a curse and keep our spirits high, then nothing happens. But we allow ourselves to be convinced that something terrible is about to happen, we are much more likely to see something bad happening to us.

We can be our own shamans by being mindful of what stories we tell and making sure that we frame our stories in a way that makes us feel good about ourselves.

There are many elements in empowered storytelling; here are a few. Changing a personal story in any way changes our emotional response to it. Any story that you're telling about your history, good or bad, is most likely based on your memory of the last time you told that particular story. So, if you change something about your emotional response to the experience, you will affect how others hear it and how you reintegrate it into your life. Very often all of this is done by changing perspective, changing focus. In, out, from another angle, from a greater perspective or more narrowly focused. Suppose you decide to tell the story of your first heartbreak from the standpoint of initiation into adulthood, as opposed to someone having done you wrong. You will significantly reduce how much hurt you feel, and you'll be happier for having done it.

The assumption here is that you can tell a story any way you like, so why not tell the story in a way that makes you feel good about yourself? It's remarkable how much latitude we have in the stories we can tell. We are free to tell any story we want or change any story. We have the ability to frame our lives any way we choose. This is powerful stuff. It is the essence of how we create our own realities.

Let's not forget that the feelings you have for yourself are your master feelings. Everything in your life flows from how you feel about yourself. Therefore, tell your stories in a way that minimizes or eliminates your victimhood. When you say that things "happened" to you, you remove your power from the equation. You allow yourself to be seen, by you and others, as powerless to do anything about what happened. Certainly there will be experiences that you (apparently) did not choose. But that's not the whole story. Your response to the experience is an essential part of the story and the piece that allows you to stay in your power.

Put your story in a context of growing, learning, and becoming more effective and powerful. It is important to feel that you are being honest with yourself about what happened, but at the same time you want to avoid a present feeling of helplessness. Helplessness may have been a factor in the story, but the *hero or heroine* overcomes helplessness in the end. So ask yourself, how did you overcome the challenges in your account or use them to your advantage?

So what is it like to change a personal story? If you have a personal story that has been hurting you for a long time, this exercise may help.

Briefly write down a story of yours that you think describes some incident or time that has dramatically affected you in a negative way. It can be just a few sentences or a couple of paragraphs, but probably not any longer than that.

Now scratch out all the adverbs and adjectives and the words that have a great deal of charge to them (this is the skinny description).

For example, your story could be "I was horribly abused as a child. I was brutally raped and forced to do disgusting things repeatedly."

First, change it to: "As a child I was often forced to do sexual things I didn't like." You have eliminated the emotionally loaded words from your description so that you can be totally honest without pushing your victim buttons.

Then change it further to, "The forced sex I had as a child taught me how to stand up for myself now as an adult, how to be aware of predatory people, and how to be compassionate towards people who are facing similar challenges."

The objective is not to deny anything, but to *put your story into a context that lets you stay in your power.* Using the ideas of empowered storytelling, find a way to look at your story that makes you feel good about yourself. You can do this with any and all of your stories about yourself.

Metaphors

One of the ways we tell stories that end up unwittingly hurting us is by using metaphors for our experience that give our power away. We want to use only metaphors that keep us empowered. We let go of the other ways of speaking about our lives.

Metaphors are figures of speech that give us a sense of what we're talking about without being literal. They are meant to suggest a resemblance and give us a way of talking about something. They are symbols and, as such, can be used very powerfully. Saying something like, "My spouse is the solid foundation of my life" is a metaphor.

One of the significant problems with metaphors, however, is that they can easily be viewed as reality and thus subtly disempower us. For example, being aware of taking on other people's negativity or energy, and then having a need to effectively release it, is a metaphor. It is a metaphor that explains the experience of feeling down or less energetic when we have been around other people who exhibit low energy, particularly with stories of blame and victimhood.

This metaphor suggests that what we are experiencing comes from outside of ourselves and that we are not responsible for having those feelings. We may take responsibility for changing those feelings, but they are a product of our interaction with someone else. The problem with this metaphor is that it portrays us as victims of energetic pollution.

Another metaphor that accounts for the experience we're having, but in a more empowered way, is that of resonance. We can also say that we have allowed our vibration to be influenced by the low vibration of another and that we have resonated with that low vibration. By acknowledging that we are the ones who are responsible for our low vibration, we then can quickly change our vibration at will and move on.

"Life is a rollercoaster." This metaphor that suggests that there are many ups and downs in life, which we have no control over. It also suggests that we just have to accept it if we want any kind of peace in our lives. However, it is disempowering. It does not acknowledge the vast amount of power we have in influencing the direction of our lives.

Most of our explanations of things are metaphors. Chakras, Heaven, and the Bluebird of Happiness are generally empowering metaphors. Personal demons and Karma are typically disempowering metaphors. Zodiac signs, for example, can make us feel either empowered or disempowered depending on how we use them. So, we need to be mindful of how our metaphors make us feel, either empowered or not.

Personal Metaphors

We each have personal metaphors that we use when thinking about ourselves. These metaphors are so ingrained now that we might have a tough time spotting them. For instance, we might think of ourselves as being blown by the wind from one disaster to the next. A better metaphor might be that we are adventuring through life with many new experiences; some we like, and some we don't.

Another unhealthy metaphor might be the familiar corporate ladder, trying to make our way up through a glass ceiling (a mildly mixed metaphor at that). This metaphor suggests that there are fixed rungs we must negotiate one at a time to get where we want to go. It also indicates that there are obstacles that we can't see that will prevent us from achieving our goals. A healthier metaphor might be that of a gardener growing a variety of delicious experiences in a vibrant and productive garden. In this garden of Life, we water and fertilize what we want to grow and pull out the weeds we don't like. The choice of metaphor affects how we feel about our experience and also our motivation to either continue or change things.

It's worth taking some time to ask yourself, "What metaphors do I use to describe my life?" Think of how you talk about yourself and see which descriptors are just adjectives or titles and which descriptors evoke some image that helps to explain you but that aren't meant to be taken literally. Just be aware of these metaphors and how they have made you feel. We can experience ourselves as a victim or a hero just by the way we use metaphors.

Here is a fun little exercise to help you with your storytelling. Write an obituary of your life up to this point—today. But this isn't an ordinary obituary that you might find in a newspaper. Make this a Sacred Obituary. Let this be the story of your sacred journey to be whole. Point out your personal triumphs, the contributions that you made to society, and the people whose lives you impacted positively. Let it include the significant points in your spiritual life. Maybe you will want to add the first time you fell in love and felt profoundly loved, or the first time your heart was broken and you felt totally unloved. Perhaps you will include a significant time when you discovered that there was a whole, vast world to be experienced—not just in the physical world, but also inside yourself, beyond your conscious mind. Perhaps you will include major things that you have done that significantly impacted your awareness of yourself and your spirit.

This is not the story of your fears, nor the story of what other people have valued in your life. This is about your journey on Earth as a human being and how you have grown and expanded through your experiences. Perhaps this is the perspective that an angel might have looking down on your life up to this point. Have fun with this, but also pay attention to how you feel as you write about your life. The feelings you engender within you as you tell your stories are what influence your life more than anything else.

Take your time doing this, but it doesn't need to be a long essay. It could be just a few paragraphs. The exercise of putting words down on paper, where you can edit it and review it, is worth the energy and time.

So how did that feel? Did you have a sense that in spite of all the ups and downs in your life, there was some order? Or perhaps you came away with a feeling of accomplishment as well as an urge to do some things differently. Whatever you felt, this is how you frame where you are today.

This next exercise is about tomorrow.

Go back inside and visualize the story that you would like to write at the end of your life. This obituary is about your life from this moment, now, to your last moment alive on Earth. In it, tell the story of the last part of your life in a way that is programming what you want to happen. This is a mighty way to feel your way into what you want and to organize your energies to get you there. So, write and talk about all the fun adventures you expect to have had. Value all the beauty you will encounter. Appreciate all the wonderful people you will meet and all the love you will both give and receive. Give thanks for all the joy you will be experiencing.

Tell the story of you in all your fullness and wholeness. Tell the story of your true authentic self in all your glory and power as you proceed into the rest of your life. *This* is the story to hang on to for the rest of your days. This process is you creating and crafting the life you want to lead. Let the other stories about your future go and let this one guide you.

As you can see, our stories are potent expressions of who we are and where we are going. It is entirely accurate to say that when we change our story, we change our lives. Coming home to ourselves is, to a considerable extent, using the metaphor of home to guide us by creating the experiences we want in our minds first, then allowing those visions to become our reality. We do this with the very best stories about ourselves that we can conceive!

Meditation 8
Taking Up My Power

Just as a fish has the power to be what it is, I have the power to be who and what I am. Just as a horse has the power to be what it is, I have the power to be who and what I am. Just as an eagle has the power to be what it is, I have the power to be who and what I am.

I am the final authority in my life. I have been given this life to explore and have adventures. It is up to me, now, how I will handle all my adventures. I am the sovereign of my personal kingdom. I am grateful for all the advisors I have, but I am the one who makes the final decisions. I do the best *I can, and that is* enough. *I do the best I can, and that is* enough.

I am the author of my life's story. I can tell the story of my past any way I like. I can tell my story with high drama and dark villains. Or I can tell my story with other people performing their profound roles in my education. There are many, many ways of telling a story. I choose one that makes me feel good about myself.

I can choose whether to be a victim of life's challenges or I can choose to be the hero of my own life. I prefer to be a hero. I choose to appreciate the heroic efforts I make to stay loving and kind in the midst of chaos. I choose to appreciate all the wonderful things I do every day.

It's Time to Come Home

I am free to focus on whatever I choose to. Whenever I can, I focus on the good things in life. I focus on the beauty that is everywhere around me. I focus on the beautiful aspects of each person I encounter. I focus on the miraculous life I am living.

I am free to be me. I have the will to be free. I have the will to take responsibility for my life. I love being free! It's one of the greatest feelings I know.

I know that I have fears and doubts, but I send them away whenever I become aware of them. They aren't my friends. My friends are trust and hope. My friends are curiosity, wonder, and awe. My friends are wisdom and joy. My friends are love and kindness.

I am the captain of my ship of life. I choose what seas I will sail into. I choose what calls from beyond I will heed and which ones I will ignore. I use my will to keep my ship safe and healthy. I use my intentions to steer by. And I use all the love in my life to keep my sails full and to propel me where I need to go.

I feel my power in my bones. I feel my power in my blood. I feel my power in my organs. I feel my power in my muscles. I feel my power in my skin. I feel my power in my eyes. I feel my power in my touch. I feel my power in my speech. I feel my power in my heart, and in the sound of my words, whether thought or spoken.

I have the power to be who and what I am. I don't have to ask anyone else for my power; I claim my power. I claim my power, now, to be who and what I am.

In addition to self-awareness, imagination, and conscience, it is the fourth human endowment—independent will—that really makes effective self-management possible. It is the ability to make decisions and choices and to act in accordance with them. It is the ability to act rather than to be acted upon, to proactively carry out the program we have developed through the other three endowments. Empowerment comes from learning how to use this great endowment in the decisions we make every day.
Stephen Covey

Chapter 9

I Accept My Power

One of the key pieces in coming home is becoming willing to accept how truly powerful we are. This means taking responsibility for our actions and their consequences. It also means taking responsibility for our thoughts and our feelings. It is this responsibility that frightens many people. This requires us to be willing to make mistakes, possibly offend some people, and face the specter of disappointment.

Learning to be self-empowered is the key to both happiness and being truly successful in all our endeavors. Personal power is the ability to accomplish the things we want to change. It is effectiveness, clarity, and satisfaction all rolled together. It is taking charge of our lives. It is managing our lives in ways that serve us best. It is authority. Another way of saying this is, power is using our energy effectively. Most importantly, personal power is a vital expression of self-love.

The primary source of our power is our feelings. As we've said, feelings are our experience of energy. When we engage our feelings and boost their intensity level we provide the charge needed to get things done. This is the key to manifestation and effectiveness. Passion is just this kind of powerful feeling.

We often need to have a mix of feelings to be successful. For instance, I may want to attract a perfect lover. Evoking the feeling of being with an ideal lover will go a long way. However, I may also need to evoke a feeling of having the power to genuinely call in that lover. And I may need to evoke a feeling of self-esteem, that I am worthy of such a lover. In this case, I might want to savor the feeling of being deliciously loved, and also call in a goddess of love, such as Aphrodite, to help me. She would also be good to identify with as a role model of worthiness.

So we work with a collection of vibrations, some of which are stronger than others. We want to bring them all into as much harmony as possible. This includes the various vibrations that we ignore or hide from because we don't know what to do with them. These are usually fears and doubts, but sometimes they are strong feelings that are intimidatingly intense. At some point, we'll have to face them all.

Most of the time we have a dominant vibration, but we don't want to forget about the others. For instance, we may have a dominant vibration of love in the presence of some special person, but we also may have a less dominant vibration, like intimidation or disorientation. There may be a third vibration of excitement at the risk of being hurt, or some other vibrations as well. These all mix to influence our choices and produce the actions we take.

Here's a little exercise that may help make this clear. Take your time doing this, and pause a little between each prompt. Stand up and start walking around. Notice how you are walking and how you are feeling. Now let yourself feel happy and walk like you're profoundly happy. Now walk like you're terribly sad. Now walk like your favorite animal. Now walk like you're outraged. Now walk like a beautiful flower. Now walk like you're going to do something you don't want to do. Now walk like you're going to a delicious feast. And now walk like everyone loves you deeply.

As you do this, be mindful of how easy it is to change how you feel. You assume each new vibration from memory.

Now here's the next level up. Walk like you are excited but also somewhat fearful. Walk like you are both very happy but also slightly sad at the same time. Walk like you are very powerful, but you also feel a little hurt.

Your vibration and your feelings are easily managed, but it takes awareness, focus and intention.

Personal power is the ability to organize our template, program, or story (pick your metaphor) to reflect our desires, plus the will to focus our energies in that direction. To use our power with confidence and competence, it's important to understand how we lose our power.

One common way that we lose power is to let other people make decisions for us. Our power is in our choices. We have the free will to choose whatever we want to. But if we allow doubt or insecurity to keep us from following our own wisdom, we tend to rely on others' ideas and opinions. This keeps us out of our own authority and disempowers us.

As we saw in Chapter 5, it doesn't matter if we are criticizing ourselves or criticizing others, we lose power. The act of saying something is wrong with someone or something is the antithesis of acceptance. It is only in accepting everything in the present moment that we have the power to change things. Anything less than acceptance blocks our ability to be effective.

Another way we lose power is to let other people criticize us. When we take the criticisms of others to heart, or even experience the fear that others will criticize us, we give others the power over our happiness. We allow these fears to hijack our focus. Instead of focusing on what we're doing right now and feeling the joys of the moment we let our imaginations envision something wrong with us—whether there is any basis for that idea or not. These thoughts activate already present thoughts and feelings of shame and guilt. As we have seen, these feelings undermine our self-esteem and self-love, and we lose our power. Until we learn to cope with and reduce these feelings, we are vulnerable to being manipulated by others.

Remember, shame is the *choice* to disapprove of some aspect of who we are and guilt is the *choice* to disapprove of something we have done, or not done. The choice to disapprove of ourselves always leads to unhappiness. To be truly empowered, it is essential to understand the decisions we are making. To make different choices we may need to change our stories, as we saw in the last chapter, and to reflect a distinctly different way of looking at our lives.

Probably the most common way that we lose power is to allow our fears and doubts to rule us. Fear and doubt sap our strength and disempower us very quickly. The more you understand that you are Spirit and thus you still exist when your body, etc. disappears, the less fear will have a hold on you. Remove fear and doubt from your focus as quickly as possible.

Fear is a present-time experience but it's about the future. Relaxing the muscles that tighten up with fear can often eliminate the potency of the fear. Think of something you fear. Now notice which muscles tighten up as you hold your focus on that fear.

Intentionally relax all the muscles involved with that fear. Now think of what brings up the fear again and see if you still react the same way. There may still be some tension, or there may be tensions elsewhere. You can repeat the process until no more tension arises with the original thought.

The more we conquer our fears, the more powerful we can become. This is why shamans do so many exercises to help them get over their fears. Each fear they overcome makes them more powerful.

Another common way we lose power is in trying to please others at the expense of our own integrity. There are lots of potential reasons for doing this, personal or emotional safety being big ones. It's quite natural and healthy to want to help other people feel better; it's the art of compassion. But, it's also important to take care of ourselves first. If we are sacrificing our energy or wellbeing for someone else, we will likely get sick and become unable to continue giving of ourselves. But when we nurture ourselves and then do what we can to help another person we stay strong and vigorous. It's the old metaphor of the airplane oxygen mask; we put ours on first before assisting someone else.

And, of course, we lose power when we try to meet other people's expectations. When we do this, essentially we are saying that their happiness is more important than our own.

Fritz Perls, the pioneer of Gestalt therapy, put it beautifully in the Gestalt Prayer:

I do my thing, and you do your thing.
I am not in this world to live up to your expectations
And you are not in this world to live up to mine.

You are you, and I am I.
And if by chance
We find each other, it's beautiful,
If not, it can't be helped.

You don't get any cosmic points for being like someone else. The best you can hope for is to be happy. *And that you get by being yourself.*

Claiming our own authority is the real key to power. Only when we claim our authority and decide for ourselves what is in our best interest can we create the lives we want. This is a conscious decision. It is the decision to be willing to override all other authorities in our lives.

We may use many other authorities for information and allow them to influence us. But to be our own authority is to say, "Yes, I will accept this idea" (perhaps with modifications), or "No, that makes no sense to me and I will let it go." It is to say, "My life is mine to choose, and the myriad decisions that I make each day are mine to make. Nobody else is in charge of my happiness. No one else is in charge of my mind."

So choose for yourself what it is that you want. This is an exercise in will—your free will. Claiming your own authority is also the greatest antidote there is to self-doubt.

Many people have such a low opinion of themselves that they would rather rely on others to tell them how to live and what to think. This means that they can never become comfortable being their own authority. That means they can never be comfortably at home in themselves.

As children, we had to accept the authority of those responsible for us, at least up to a point. As we became adults most of us were never shown that it was now time to be our own authority. New parents have to learn this fairly quickly, in the midst of their self-doubt. They have to make significant decisions with long-term repercussions based on what limited information they have. Out of necessity, they have to be the authority for their children whether they know what they're doing or not.

Just the same, becoming our own authority is not something that most political, religious, or social institutions encourage. They would prefer to be the authorities in our lives. But, we cannot fully become who we are, and thus come home, until we do accept ourselves as our primary authority.

To be your own authority means to permit yourself to make "mistakes." You need to have the freedom to do things that don't end up working out as well as you would have liked them to. You will have to try things out and learn for yourself what works and what doesn't. In other words, you are both the authority and the experimenter. Remember, you don't have to know everything. You are just the one in charge of the experiments.

Being your own authority doesn't mean that you don't ask for advice, help, insight, or inspiration. Asking for these things is always a good idea. No matter how good all of that wisdom is, however, you're the one who needs to choose to accept it, or not, to whatever degree you feel is appropriate. You may hold things in the I'm-not-so-sure category. Or you may say, "Yup, that's for me!" The important thing here is that you are the final authority. Don't let anyone or anything shake you from that. The buck stops with you.

The primary step in becoming empowered is to claim the authority to choose how we use our focus. First, we need to recognize that we are in charge of what we focus on, or at least we can be. There is great power in moving our focus around; our attention directs our personal energy. By accepting that we have the ability to direct our energy we vastly increase our effectiveness.

Second, we want to become aware of how we feel about what we are currently focused on. Since everything we choose to do is motivated by a desire to feel better than we currently do, we need to monitor whether or not our choices are working for us. That entails paying attention to how we are feeling right now.

And third, once we know how we're feeling, we can then choose how we want to feel, and whether that is different in some way or not. It is from that perspective that we can focus on that which will give us the feeling we desire.

Not long ago I resigned from a volunteer post that I had proudly taken up only a few months before. The situation turned out to be entirely different from my perception of it, and I felt the need to change course quickly. Some people were disappointed with me, some were angry, and others acknowledged a smart decision on my part.

What was most noticeable in people's reactions was their surprise that I had acted so suddenly and resolutely by going in a direction entirely contrary to what was expected. I had just written a new chapter in my life story in a way that was my own, without reference to anyone else's opinions or pressure. This, to me, is an expression of personal power: the ability to choose for oneself and to act on it. It is an act of claiming one's own authority.

When we are making the decisions for ourselves, we combine our desires, our wisdom, our awareness of our capabilities and limitations, and the input and help of Spirit (if we have asked for it). Sure, that may boil down to our opinion. But, I think our opinions should matter more than the opinions of anyone else. We, after all, have to live with our opinions and the results of our actions. It is by taking responsibility for our lives that we can navigate our way to the happy and satisfying experiences we're looking for.

So how might we break down personal authority into its constituent pieces? Let's take a look at what most of them are.

The most prominent element is clarity of desire: "I am clear about what it is that I want." If we don't know what we want it doesn't matter who's making the decisions in our life. One choice is as good as another. But the moment we decide that we want something our whole focus can go in that direction. And since it is our desire, no one else will ever understand it the way we do—or needs to.

Another element of our authority is to acknowledge that we have a birthright to ask for what we want and to go for it. This is an acceptance of our ability to be free as human beings if indeed we choose to claim that freedom. This is to say that once we have elected to take our place as whole beings on Earth, we deserve to receive what it is that we desire, so long as we do no harm to others. We may not find it manifesting precisely as we had imagined, but it will likely be very close.

The third element of our authority is that of responsibility. We lose a lot of our power when we blame other people or situations for whatever it is that we don't like. We lose our happiness then, too. When we say, "I, alone, am responsible for my choices," we are letting go of all blame. It's like the difference between a Paint-By-Number painting and creating a work of art from our own imagination. We can't be fully creative if we are looking over our shoulder to see what others are thinking about what we're doing. We need to be able to say, "This is how I choose this thing, in this moment, whatever the consequences may be."

This is especially important when it comes to how we will live in our bodies and use our sexuality. There seems to be no end of opinions about how we should be taking care of our bodies, what appropriate body shapes are and what are not, and which expressions of sexuality are okay and which are not. This element of our authority means the difference between continually living in shame or in freedom.

When we take up our authority, we are claiming our own sovereignty. We are the divine rulers of our lives. We become the ones who decide if it is to be a life of joy and happiness or one of misery. The sovereign says, "I, alone, am responsible for my happiness."

So, permit yourself to make "mistakes" and to do things that don't work out as well as you would have liked them to. In other words, be both the authority and the experimenter. You don't have to know everything. You are just the one in charge of the experiments. The more experiments you make, the more you will learn and the wiser you will become. When you are genuinely empowered, you make all of the decisions regarding your life. And that's the path to happiness!

Intention and Will

Intention and will are very close, but they are not exactly the same thing. Intention is a form of focus in which it is assumed that our will is in agreement. Our will, however, is that part of us that makes things happen. It is a primal part of us that decides to do anything, or nothing; whether it is to make coffee in the morning, sunbathe, or to go after a new career. It is the link between motivation and action.

The difference can be seen in the two sentences: "I am going out to get a quart of milk" (intention) and "I bring more milk into my life" (will). Another example is: "I am going to find the right job for myself" (intention) and "Perfect job, come to me!" (a command of will).

We use both will and intention all the time, and the more we use them, the more powerful we become. We take our authority and use our focus to produce the results we want with our intention and our will.

Intentions work best when we are very concise. We mentioned it when we were talking about authority: "I am clear about what it is that I want." Without that clarity we are wasting our time. Remember, once we get where we wanted to go, we can always change direction and go somewhere else next.

So, we don't have to get it perfectly right the first time. A simple sentence that carries great emotional weight is best. Instead of a statement like, "I want to do the kind of work that feels good to me and makes a difference in other people's lives," try "I help others in whatever way I can in a manner that is also satisfying to me."

Setting your intention is a choice to align your mind and heart to be, or act, in a way that supports a desired outcome. Forming a positive intention tells the Universe that you are serious about exploring or accomplishing something specific and sets everything in motion. It creates an energetic map for reality to follow.

It's valuable to take some time to carefully craft what you would like to experience. Write it down, say it out loud, feel it as deeply as you can, and repeat it as you start your actions. Clearly describe to yourself where you want your experience to take you or what you want it to provide for you.

A strong intention helps you to stay focused. Without an intention, or with a weak one, it's easy to wander off and zone out. An intention adds emotional energy that significantly helps us to stay fully on track.

Intentions can be about simple little things that people want to do or be that don't involve great efforts. For instance, some people make their intentions for the day as soon as they wake up. Other intentions can be about significant life plans, as in intending to go to college or trade school, intending to lose weight, or intending to do the work to get to know themselves better.

The idea behind intentions is to concentrate our personal energy consciously in one direction. A wish is in this same family, though not so strong. An expectation is also in this family and even stronger than intention. However, expectations can be dangerous if not used properly. Expectations of other people run afoul of free will and thus aren't particularly useful. We looked at expectations in Chapter 6.

Will is a kind of command. It tells the body to do certain specific things, like get out of bed, hold off urinating until we get to a bathroom, or run a little more and then we're done. Will is also how we visualize. We will specific pictures to come together. We modify these visions with our will and see the instantaneous results of our will before our inner eyes. If we energize these visualizations with our feelings and give them enough focus (energy), we will manifest them in reality.

Sometimes will comes before intention, as in willing the vision and then clearly stating your intention to bring this something about. Sometimes intention comes before will, as in having the intention to send ailing Aunt Agatha healing energy and then willing that energy to flow to her.

Honor your uniqueness more than your conformity

As we all know, we're social beings. We need to belong and feel that we have a place in the world. For many people that means being a part of a group: a family, a tribe, a nation, or a religion. This is especially true when we are young. Nevertheless, at some point we find that we are not exactly like the ideal of that group nor hold the same values. We notice that we have become different, and that difference can cause us trouble. Discovering that we have an individuality, a uniqueness, and some eccentricity can be confusing and possibly dangerous. Many groups dislike those who are different (though each member is likely hiding their own inevitable differences). As John F. Kennedy put it, "Conformity is the jailer of freedom and the enemy of growth."

In this light, we need to be okay with who we are as we go through this process of individuating. While this happens most strongly in young adulthood, it continues for the rest of our lives. It then becomes essential to find ways to be safe to be who we are. We need to find places, friends, and work that allow us to freely be ourselves.

This entails the need to let go of other people's definitions of us. It's natural for all of us to form some idea of who someone else is. We don't want to have to continually strain to understand the deeper aspects of each person. But that leads to a simplified and superficial understanding of those around us. Unfortunately, being as busy as we think we're supposed to be, that may be all we have time for.

This leads us to project our simplifications onto the people we're dealing with. And if it's us that are being simplified and made superficial, and we change at all, then the already distorted vision of us becomes merely a cartoon.

At the same time, other people will want us to be who they think we are. And their annoyance that we aren't who or what they think we are is something they will blame on us. Crazy, isn't it? But it happens all the time.

We can't afford to pay much attention to what other people think about us. They have their own subjective experience of us, and we're not responsible for that. This is true for opinions, expectations, and judgments. It is an act of power to let go of concern around what others know or what they think of us. They are living in their own reality, and we can feel blessed that our reality is different.

However, we need to be willing to endure other people's choices to be disappointed with who we are now. If we maintain our authenticity, though, either they will come around and like us for the new way we are, or we will be better off when they choose to leave our lives.

Here's a little visualization to illustrate this individualization and our reintegration.

Picture yourself as a little water droplet high up in the sky. Way, way up there you're in the company of millions of other tiny water droplets. You have lots of company and nothing to worry about. [Pause] Except that it's getting cold. It's getting very cold. It's getting so cold that, *bang!* You suddenly transform into a beautiful snowflake. *All* of you former water droplets have now changed into snowflakes. And you start to fall very, very slowly toward the Earth.

On your way down you look around and notice that each of you is slightly different from all the rest. In one or more ways, you have characteristics that you don't seem to share with any of your fellow snowflakes. None of you is more or less beautiful. You are all exquisitely dazzling, just different from each other. You're each unique. Isn't it amazing how different you can be from each other and still be amazingly gorgeous?

As you float down, you can also be aware of the splendor of this journey. You know that it won't go on forever. But it is so much fun and exciting while it lasts!

Eventually, you come to rest in a pile of other lovely snowflakes. You know that at some point you will all return to water droplets. But at this moment, give thanks for the opportunity to have been a magnificent snowflake, unique and wonderful in your own way, for a while.

We take back our power by taking up our authority and being okay with being responsible for our entire lives. Not only does this mean making all the choices about our actions, it also means choosing our vibration and the emotional stance we take each day.

Remember when Nelson Mandela was leaving the prison he had been in for so many years? He was determined to forgive all the people involved in his imprisonment. If he hadn't, he believed he'd continue to live in prison. He chose the vibration of forgiveness because it provided him with a vital implement of power—and the freedom that comes with that choice.

Meditation 9

I Am Comfortable With My Sexuality

My body's desires are amazing! They are such strong feelings that seem to come out of nowhere. They overwhelm me at times. Do the birds and the bees feel this so intensely?

I love the feeling of being sexually attracted to someone. I'm often surprised by whom or what I'm attracted to. I don't have to be afraid of these powerful feelings. I know they are all quite natural.

I don't have to act on all my feelings. In fact, I'm certain that many of these feelings I don't want to act on. But I can let myself feel all of these feelings, anyway. I know that feelings can't hurt me but that resisting them can.

My body is my friend. It knows how to be a body better than my mind does. I may not understand what my body is doing or what it wants. But I know that it is always working for my benefit. All I have to do is take care of my body and help it meet its needs safely.

Some people find my body attractive, and some people don't. My love of myself is not dependent on other people's opinions. My body feels good, and I can enjoy the great gift of sensuality no matter what other people think. I love my body, and my body loves me!

My pleasures don't have to be like anyone else's. I know that I'm a little different from my friends. Each of them is different from the others, too. We all have our own sexualities, and that's as it should be. My sexual interests and pleasures are my own. Just like my face, my sense of humor, and what music I like, my sexuality is unique and distinct. I am my own sexual being.

I love the sense of fun I have with sex! There's such a lively joy there! In the midst of such intensity, I get to be playful and free. I get to roll around in deep intimacy and frolic with another being. I get to tease and be teased to my heart's content.

I love the build-up of intensity. Each moment, each stroke, each touch invites me to relax more and give in to this enormous pleasure. With each breath, waves of energy build and the excitement intensifies. It doesn't matter what my style of sex is; this experience is exquisite!

And, if and when an orgasm comes, I surrender most profoundly. The energy consumes me. I feel that the curtains of separation are thrown back, and I can sense All-That-Is. There are no words for this deliciousness!

I know that all pleasures come to an end, but I love to prolong the feelings I have inside. I savor each delightful sensation. I cherish this magnificent feeling of well-being. And I love this openness to love. I love, and that is enough!

When I go to sleep tonight, I will think about some of the beautiful pleasures I have had and let them keep me company as I sleep. Whatever thoughts, feelings, and experiences I have are all wonderful, and I am grateful for them all!

Your emotions are your inner guidance system. They alone will let you know whether you are living in an environment of biochemical health or in an environment of biochemical distress. Understanding how your thoughts and your emotions affect every single hormone and cell in your body, and knowing how to change them in a way that is health-enhancing, gives you access to the most powerful and empowering health-creating secret on earth.
Christiane Northrup

Intelligence is present everywhere in our bodies; our own inner intelligence is far superior to any we can try to substitute from the outside.
Deepak Chopra

Chapter 10

My Body Is My Faithful Friend

One of the most important ways of being compassionate with ourselves is to treat our bodies with the same kindness and consideration that we would treat a dear friend or beloved. Our bodies work hard every day to please us and do the things that we want to do. We ask our bodies to work, often at significant discomfort, for long hours on projects that only the conscious mind finds value in. We tell our bodies what to do and then shame them when they don't conform to ideas we, or others, have about how they should look and behave. This is how a slave gets treated, and there is nothing whatsoever that is compassionate about slavery!

It makes much more sense to treat our body as a friend—a very dear, loving friend. Since the stress that we create with our mind causes most, if not all, of the illness and discomfort in our bodies, it is not our body's fault that we get sick. That illness is the result of conflicts and tensions in the mind that have repercussions in the body. There is no point in getting mad at our body for not cooperating with our mind to perform one more unpleasant task that is ultimately injurious to our whole being. Becoming upset that a cold or worse has laid us up only adds to our stress, and that in turn requires more rest. Not only is our body our friend, but it is *always* on our side. That is, it is always working for our overall benefit. Once we understand that, it becomes much easier to let our mind and our body work together as a team, instead of fighting each other at every turn. But that requires cooperation between the two, something that may be a bit foreign for some of us.

Have you ever had an intense conversation with your body? I mean one of those heart-to-hearts that holds nothing back. It's a conversation where you, as conscious mind, really need to listen to you as a physical body. This "body-mind" has a very different perspective on life than does your conscious mind. To be genuinely compassionate to yourself, you need to extend that compassion to every part of your being, and that includes the body.

Just for starters, close your eyes (after reading these few sentences) and ask your body with just your thought, what it would like you to know right now. Listen for whatever comes into your mind. It may not come immediately, just be patient. And once you feel that you hear something, pay attention without judgment or defense. You may not like what it has to say, but it is vital for your long-term enjoyment.

Okay. Did you hear or sense a message? This practice isn't a hard thing to do, but it is so very valuable. In classes, when we do this, I often hear people exclaiming how grateful their bodies were that they were *finally* being listened to.

We are surrounded by messages that our bodies should be this way or that, and that particular diets, exercise programs, and treatments are what we absolutely need. But no one thinks to ask the body what it thinks or wants. Just like a child, the body-mind has its own needs and desires. For one thing, the body-mind is thoroughly focused on pleasure. That is, it always wants to feel good in some way. Sure, sex is wonderful, but there are lots of other pleasures that it would enjoy. A walk in nature, a hot bath on a cold day, a glass of lemonade or a beer, or a friendly smile shared getting coffee are all significant pleasures for a body. These sorts of joys, small by themselves but huge in the aggregate, keep the body happy and ready to do what our mind has in store for the day.

Since the body is always on the lookout for pleasure, it avoids pain as much as possible. And stress is a pain. So, to be kind to our bodies we need to prevent all stresses and strains, as best we can, and especially the effects of fear. Is there a way to have a stress-free life short of lying in a hammock on the beach drinking a piña colada? Well, maybe not stress-free, but we can certainly enormously reduce the stress in our body.

The first way to reduce stress in our body is to stop criticizing it. Compassion means to accept everything and do whatever seems possible to alleviate suffering. Our bodies hate criticism just as any conscious mind does. Remember, the idea behind criticism is to make things better by being aware of shortcomings. It doesn't work. It only creates more stress and resistance to change. So criticizing the body *in any way* not only doesn't work, it creates more problems. Going against the prevailing winds of fashion and fads takes a lot of energy and courage. But your body will thank you for it, and in ways that will make you much happier.

The second way to reduce stress is to pay attention to what your body likes and doesn't like. While this may sound obvious, the body doesn't consistently like any one thing. It may, for instance like chocolate cake often. But there are likely times when it wants a carrot, instead. And when the carrot is finished, it may want chocolate cake or maybe something else. The point is, as with a child or a lover, we need to be mindful of the changing desires, whims if you will, of the body to keep it happy.

Now there will probably be desires for things that we need to say "no" to; a fast but expensive car, for example. The body's desire for sex with someone who is in a monogamous relationship with someone else would be another example. But the point here, as always, is that underlying every desire for something is a desire for a feeling. The body wants feelings—good feelings. You can do things that feel good, but you can also imagine things that feel good. The body is generally happy either way as long as the imagination is strong enough. The power of imagined feelings is what makes strong anticipation often sap the excitement of the real thing later on.

Another aspect to be mindful of here is that happy, loving thoughts about other people also make the body feel good. Whereas criticism of any kind makes the body feel bad, compliments and appreciation make it feel good. Any kind of beauty makes the body feel good. And laughter is one of the very best ways to love your body. It's worth being aware of how quickly the body reacts to thoughts, both positive and negative thoughts. If we intentionally hold affirmative, constructive thoughts, we keep the body happy.

Getting to know our individual body is the easiest way to grow out of the shame we have been taught to hold in our body. Just as with any friend, we want to see what's going on in the life of our body. Looking at all parts of our body, with compassion, is an essential first step. This may require the use of a mirror to look at parts that we cannot see without some assistance. We may also want to look at our bodies from different perspectives, so that we can accept how anyone else might be seeing us. Our bodies are unique, but they also have similarities to other people's bodies. Looking to see the similarities and the differences—and accepting both—makes it easier to genuinely love our bodies.

For some of us, this next step may be particularly challenging, but if that's the case it will be the most healing. Letting other people see your naked body, even strangers, can be enormously therapeutic and liberating. Most of our shame about our body is focused on what we imagine others will say, if they only knew our secret about what our body really looks like. But once we let other people see what our body actually looks like there is nothing left to fear. It can be an enormous letdown when there is no reaction from others when we finally reveal ourselves. And when we allow ourselves to look at the naked bodies of others, we can easily notice that we all have aspects of our bodies that don't match up with some externally dictated notion of how a body should look.

When we let go of that fear of other people's reactions to the sight of our body, then we are free to enjoy the feeling of the sun, the water, and the breeze on all of our skin. The pleasure of this openness and the sensations that come with it are far more nurturing and healthy than hiding from any potential criticism or derision that we might imagine.

Taking this a bit further, it is time then to get to know how the body has undergone all the transformations, trials, excitements, and marvels of life. At some point, when nothing is likely to interrupt this exercise, sit or lie comfortably, close your eyes, and ask from within to be shown your life's history from your *body's* perspective. I suggest that you ask the story to start somewhere around conception and go all the way up to the present moment.

This is not the mind's story, it is the body's story, so this is about experiences and feelings without judgment or analysis. Just see what comes up. There is no right or wrong here, it is just your body's perspective on things that you may or may not remember. Take your time, but don't force anything. You're getting to know your friend better. So listen and care about what it reveals to you.

Take some time to digest what you've just learned from your body. There is great value in recognizing the intrinsic value of your body's point of view. Your body has a life of its own and it's experiencing things all the time. While your mind is off gallivanting around in the dream world when you sleep, your body is going through its processes of rejuvenation and integration. It's in the present moment 24/7, whether the mind is there or not. Its experiences will always be somewhat different, and that difference needs to be respected.

Since we tend to identify with our conscious minds more than with our bodies, we have a mental bias against our bodies. This is as unwise as it is unfair. We, as human beings, are multilayered and our bodies are an essential layer. Obviously, there would be no life without the body. But, more than that, most of life is experiences and most of experience is feeling. And it is the body that experiences those feelings. So, essentially, the body is doing most of the living. Our minds just make commentary!

Because we are so complex and hold so many conflicting thoughts and beliefs, it's quite natural that our bodies and our minds will come into conflict. It's important to remember what our ultimate goals are as we step in to resolve these conflicts. If we have decided that doing our duty is the most important thing in life, then we have a specific kind of relationship with the body. If we have chosen to regard only spiritual aspirations as most valuable, then we have a different relationship with the body. However, if we have chosen something like happiness, joy, or love as our primary value, the relationship of the mind with the body is that of team members.

What this means is that if this is the road we've chosen, the mind's job is to serve the body in the best possible way. While the mind is in charge of making choices, it is the body that primarily experiences everything. And, since each spiritual experience has a bodily component, it feels exceedingly wonderful (if it didn't we wouldn't be interested), and the mind's job includes taking care of our spiritual needs.

Your body is healthiest when it is happy. What makes your body happy may not be the same as what makes someone else's body happy. So diet, exercise, and rest are individual things that need to be discussed by both sides. We resolve conflicts between the body and the conscious mind by conversation and respect for each side's points of view.

One simple way of encouraging this dialogue is to pretend that your conscious mind and your body-mind are both sitting down at a table with you. You, as mediator, want to make them both feel equally honored and respected. You want to be sure that they understand that you value both points of view.

Then ask one or the other to start, it doesn't matter which one goes first, and state what the problem is from their point of view. For example, the mind might be complaining that the body isn't willing to work late into the evening on a business project. Then, ask the other one to state the problem from their point of view. The body might say that the work was excessively tiring and boring. It needs exercise, food, and rest but it wasn't getting enough of any of them.

Having stated what the problem looks like from each individual point of view, have each side, in turn, state what they see as *their* contributions to the problem. The mind might say that perhaps it was making this project more important than the overall happiness of the whole being. The body might say that it wasn't making any effort to provide the extra energy needed to complete the project and that, perhaps, if it did, it might be more willing to endure, temporarily, the hardships of getting it done.

The final step would be to ask each side to offer solutions to the conflict. The mind might find some way of rewarding the body for the extra effort requested of it. The body might say that it would look for more ways of enjoying the fruits of the labor. In other words, let the mind and the body contribute to the solution of the conflict rather than imposing the will of one on the other.

The mind's motivation is accomplishment. It wants the satisfaction of triumph over challenges and the sense of succeeding in something important. If you want to motivate the mind, find a task that is not too hard, but hard enough to be interesting. The body's motivation is pleasure. Everything revolves around feeling good. If you want the body to do more, reward it appropriately. It is perfectly happy to negotiate deals. And nothing rewards the body like fun.

The Power of Fun

Recently, I had a lot of fun with some friends at a dinner. We laughed over our various plights and oversights. We enjoyed tales of success and near-success. We savored delicious food in an atmosphere of camaraderie and amusement. The following day I had fun going to the botanical garden by myself and photographing beautiful flowers and trees. Later, I had fun solving a particularly difficult Sudoku puzzle.

I experienced fun in all of these activities, yet they were each unique. We all know the experience of fun, and most of us treasure those times of fun. But then, all too often, we get serious and go back to taking care of the problems of life. So what makes something fun? And why aren't we always choosing things that are fun?

The dictionary tells us that fun is the experience of enjoying something or being amused. My experience of fun is a lot more than that! For me, fun is something that I experience in my heart. It's not the same feeling as love, but it's close. It is a feeling that I associate with being alive. The core of my very being gets excited.

Anticipating a great pleasure is exciting, as is doing something that is borderline dangerous. But fun is a different kind of excitement. It is an excitement of freedom, the freedom to be who we are. When we are having fun, we let go of fears and doubts about how we might be perceived by others or how we "should" be acting. We are spontaneous and open; we are expressing our authentic nature without holding back.

Somehow, though, other things that aren't particularly fun seem to be more important. These are the things that "have" to be done, the ones that we do to take care of the necessities of life. Sure, fun is nice, but only after everything else is done. Or, at least, so goes the thinking—duty first, etc.

The unfortunate thing about duty is that it makes us slaves. Our free will is largely abandoned to fulfill the dictates of our duty. It isn't that what we consider our duty is bad in some way. It's how we look at it. As long as we're treating these things that are to be done as necessities, we reluctantly do them with the hope of finishing them quickly.

Suppose that we choose to do things differently. Suppose that we decide to look at our choices as a matter of which things give us more pleasure, or fun, or love. Suppose that we make pleasure, fun, and love the basis of our personal ethic. This is the kind of perspective that restores our freedom. It's an act of will to shape how we are thinking, to view our tasks in the context of a strategy to maximize our pleasure.

When we make choices based on what will add to our joy and fun, we cultivate a sense of vitality and a true motivation to accomplish what we've set out to do. In this sense, fun is a nutrient. Fun is to the body what ecstasy is to the soul. Fun is an essential act of self-love. We need to provide our bodies with sufficient fun, of whatever kind, to keep them happy and healthy.

Coming Home to Our Sexuality

Perhaps the most challenging and perplexing dimension of our bodies is our sexuality. The intense desires and feelings involved with our sexual experiences are so powerful and the cultural attitudes towards them are so confusing and conflicting. It's no surprise that we come into adulthood with a broad variety of feelings of shame and guilt. As long as we consider the body as a minor player in life, we dishonor the robust, fiery, and sometimes violent energies that are natural aspects of living in a body. Riding the wild animal that is our essence is tough enough without a chorus of voices telling us that we should or should not do or feel certain things. Finding our way back home requires us to come to terms with *all* that's involved in our sexuality.

One way of looking at sex, besides the obvious pleasure and potential for intimate connection, is to see it as a call to wholeness. Why do we feel compelled to seek these powerful connections with others? Why are we willing to sacrifice so much money, freedom, self-respect, or personal time, to have a fleeting orgasm or two? What drives us to place so much emphasis in our lives on something that, while enjoyable, is messy, awkward, loud, and thoroughly unruly?

A call to wholeness is the irresistible demand of parts of us to be reintegrated into the fullness of our being. The impulse of some women to have children is a call to wholeness. It is the sense that this something must be done if we are to feel complete. For others this call is for adventure, business success, fame, or inner peace.

In this same way, sex is often a compulsion to connect with some part of our soul that is seemingly missing. For many people it is about connecting to the opposite gender, and to explore the world for a short time from a radically different perspective. For others, this connection needs to be made with the same gender to explore parts of us that haven't been fully explored or integrated.

There are so many ways that we get turned on by others, all of which are valid and valuable explorations, that categorizing them makes little sense. But if we look at sex, then, as a way for us to investigate ourselves, it becomes a powerful tool for inner knowledge.

Dr. Jack Morin wrote a book called *The Erotic Mind* in which he discussed his observation that each of us has a dominant erotic fantasy that guides our erotic, and thus sexual, lives. He called these dominant fantasies core erotic themes. And these themes tell us a lot about ourselves. Very often they are keys to our sexual healing.

Making love, masturbating, getting laid are all very pleasurable, at least usually, and that pleasure is a great impetus to do more of it. But what gets overlooked mostly is sex on the soul level. What are we trying to accomplish at this deeper level? I suggest that it is a craving to enjoy that hidden pleasure of feeling complete and whole.

This is a pleasure that mystifies us in both its nature and its intensity. It often feels like an obsession and seems to be a fixation. The passion that arises is often frighteningly uncontrollable. When observing it from the outside, this could easily be called manic behavior. From a more compassionate view we might ask, "What need does this behavior address?"

When we are talking about coming home to ourselves, we need to look at all aspects of our being as loved parts of ourselves. There are no "bad" features of us, just parts we like less than others. Sometimes the body has to develop dramatic means of getting the attention of our conscious mind. Each one of these "symptoms" is a way for the body to attempt to solve a problem. The mind's job is not to fight the body for doing what it's doing; it is to find out what problem the body is addressing and find a better way of solving that problem.

So what is the body/mind/soul up to when we desperately need to jump someone's bones? If we pursue the notion that it is our core erotic theme that is driving things, then we must view what we are feeling from that perspective. That is, since it is created in our inner world, we must view it in those terms.

An erotic theme of submission may be a cry for a balance of giving and taking power, but it may also be a simple desire to submit to a higher being of loving authority, like a god or goddess. The eroticism of *Wonder Woman* is about this type of submission. An erotic theme of exhibitionism might well be the hunger to simply be seen as a human being without the numbing effects of shame.

A yearning for sexual connection to underage people could easily be a desire to connect to one's own youth, and a sexual freedom and innocence that was denied at that time. Erotic fantasies revolving around masochistic abuse can be a deep craving to learn how to take back one's power and be in control of one's body and sexuality.

The kinds of feelings and longings that occur, sadly often called perversions, are ways that our inner being is trying to heal and become whole again. So the act of looking at our core erotic theme as a signpost pointing to our next level of healing is a powerful instrument at our disposal.

Here's a simple exercise to illustrate this idea. Close your eyes and call in your favorite erotic fantasies. Can you find one or more common themes that are in them all, or in most of them? Then, ask to see what aspect of your being feels incomplete without this theme. (It doesn't matter who or what you ask; the magic of this kind of thing is in just asking.) In other words, what problem, issue, or deeper knowledge does this erotic theme address? If nothing comes quickly, relax and go into yourself more deeply. Let the answer come to you. You don't have to share this erotic theme with anyone else. But do explore it thoroughly as more than just a fantasy. Look at it as very useful information about who you really are.

Remember, it takes a lot of courage to look at yourself to any great depth. Please be as compassionate in this as you can. And it takes at least as much bravery to accept what you see.

Your Sexual History

Nowhere is the understanding of how our stories map out our lives so important as in the realm of our stories about our sexuality. For many of us, our picture of our own power and sense of identity is intimately tied to our sexual history. A history is, of course, a story, created and modified to suit our needs at the time. So we may have story elements that have to do with being victims of some kind of abuse or betrayal. Our entire being is then influenced by these aspects of the story.

If we are to heal these aspects of our personhood, that is, bring them back in to be owned and loved, we need to not only look at them but to see them in the context of the rest of our lives. For instance, if I find that I was raped as a young teenager and have felt scarred by that event ever since, it behooves me to look at all the other times I have felt victimized. To heal is to move from being a victim to one of triumph over adversity. Acknowledging a pattern of victimhood points to a set of beliefs that are being played out over and over until the pattern is changed. Once I recognize that I was a contributing player in the chapters of my history, I can take back my power, harvest the lessons from these experiences, and make different choices in the future.

Seldom do we put down all our stories in one place, particularly our stories about sex. This is a good way of putting these stories in perspective, and a way of seeing which stories most need healing. This next exercise might be emotionally challenging, but it is well worth doing when the time and space allow you to process these events.

Write your sexual history from beginning to end (so far!). In this history, be sure to provide details from each of the three perspectives: your mind, your body, and your spirit. For example, you might say, "I knew it was a sin to have sex with this person, but my body felt like it was on fire with lust, and I had this strong feeling that this person would complete me in some way." While the intense eroticism of these experiences may seem like porn, it is how we have held them in our bodies and minds that hold the great value of this work. How have these stories shaped the way we make our decisions, chosen new mates, hold others in our value system, and how we now see our abilities as we move into the future?

When you have finished writing your sexual history to your satisfaction, you might want to simply appreciate this enormous adventure your life has been, particularly the chapters that involved the immense impact of sexual energy on you. Remember, there's no good and bad, right and wrong. It's just your life, as complicated, confusing, glorious, and amazing as anyone else's.

While you have a natural sexual response in your body, what is erotic and a turn on is based on your beliefs and attitudes. Your erotic story creates your erotic experience. The invitation here is to pay attention to your stories and especially to feed the ones that help you feel good. You are free to explore the sexual realm to the degree you permit yourself to do so. Whatever sexual limits you have, you have either placed there yourself or consented to.

It may be that you don't actually want to manifest in physical reality all of your sexual and erotic desires. Some of them may be dangerous, inappropriate for you or the potential partner, or harmful to other aspects of your being. For example, you may not want to actually have intercourse on the edge of a cliff at midnight, or be ravished by a wild animal, or be whipped while tied naked to the mast of a sailing ship.

But that doesn't mean that these desires shouldn't be explored. Each of these desires is a part of your life exploration. Experimenting with each of these feelings brings you closer to who you are. Eventually, it will be important to integrate all of your desires into your sense of who you are and accept yourself in your entirety. Another way of putting this is to say that you are claiming the freedom to be fully yourself sexually and erotically, to be free of judgment, free of shame, and free of inhibition.

Innocence is the absence of shame and of ideas about who we *should* be. It's worth taking the time to see if you can find a sense of innocence within you, and to explore your sexual impulses, desires, and turn-ons from a place of innocence within. There is immense freedom in this innocence. Take the time to let your hidden, perhaps forbidden, desires show themselves.

Your pleasure is a function of what you're paying attention to. If you are focused on loving yourself and your partner, then you will expand your love. If you are focused on fears and doubts about your performance, either giving or receiving, then you will ruin the pleasure experience. Any distractions of memories or things that might be will also ruin the pleasure experience. A simple focus on what is happening in the moment is the only way to allow you to enjoy the situation.

The Tantric text, *The Vijñānabhairava*, while talking here in this quote about sex as such, is a marvelous inventory of savoring inner experiences to the point of divine connection:

At the start of the union, be in the fire of the energy released by intimate sensual pleasure. Merge into the divine Shakti and keep burning in space, avoiding the ashes at the end.
These delights are in truth those of the Self.

(From *Tantra Yoga, le Vijñānabhairava Tantra* that is translated with commentary by Daniel Odier, translated from the French version of Daniel Odier by Jeanric Meller.)

Coming home to ourselves includes honoring the great joys of our sensuality. Not only are there no bad parts of us, *all* the parts of us are aspects of All-That-Is. Every part of us that is worthy of love and exploration.

Margot Anand, the famed author of the book *The Art of Sexual Ecstasy,* and others, created a powerful and enchanting affirmation that sums up these ideas:

It's Time to Come Home

From now on, I will be responsible for my life. I take back all the power that I have given away out of a desire to conform, please others, or do the "proper" thing. I no longer delegate my power to parents, to teachers, to priests, to politicians, to opinion polls, or to the media.

I take back the power to determine my own future. In particular, I will be responsible for my own love life. I reclaim the power to honor my sexuality as the deepest source of my creative energy, as a motor for my transformation. I take back the right to use this sexual motor to become a fully orgasmic human being, knowing that this is my door to sexual magic and the key to transforming my entire life.

Meditation 10
I Want My Body to Be Happy

*M*y *body has had an incredible life. It has experienced an enormous amount of feelings, a vast number of exquisite encounters with each of the senses, and progressed through dramatic and complex growth stages. It has borne the wounds of injury and heartache. And it has given me the creaturehood in which I get to explore the miracle of life. I love my body and all the wonders that make it up.*

I love all the beauty my eyes have seen. They like looking at beautiful things and people. My eyes relax and savor the details of beauty. They feel good when I take the time to look at things in a pleasurable way.

I love all the wonderful things my ears get to hear. My ears enjoy listening to the many things that are around me. My ears feel good when I listen to things I like.

My nose loves to smell beautiful things. There are so many things that my nose has enjoyed over the years. Many of my memories are intimately tied to the smells connected to them. My nose feels good when I smell delightful things.

My lips have had some of my best times. There have been genuinely epic experiences where my lips have met other lips. I love how my lips both express how I feel and receive the intimate feelings of others. I love how my lips feel.

My tongue has had some of the most glorious experiences of my life. It has tasted so many exceptional things and has experienced a vast variety of exquisite sensations. Every day my tongue is the gateway to many of the most important aspects of my life. I love making my tongue happy.

Taking food into my body feels fantastic. I love how good I feel when I feel nourished. My body feels alive and healthy when it is nurtured by good food. Even getting rid of the waste feels good. I love the feelings I get when my body is lovingly fed.

It is a huge blessing to breathe deeply and easily. I love to feel the air coming in and going out of my lungs. Feeling the pleasure of my lungs relaxes me and centers me. I love the feeling of breathing.

My body loves to move. Sometimes it likes to dance, or run, or walk. Sometimes it likes to stretch and exercise in specific ways. And sometimes it likes to gently snuggle and cuddle. I love how my body moves in so many pleasurable ways.

And my body loves to be touched. My scalp loves to be massaged. Having fingers gently rub all over my scalp is a wonderful thing. Perhaps my ears enjoy being rubbed as well. Feeling hands and fingers move over my skin, both with a very light touch and with some deeper pressure feels fantastic.

I love the feelings I get in my genitals. It feels terrific when I touch myself, and I love how nurtured I feel when I touch my genitals. I also love it when other people's hands lovingly touch my genitals. It is one of my very favorite feelings, and I am thankful for all the wonderful feelings I've had with my genitals.

I also love all the feelings I can have in and around my groin area. There is such delicious sensitivity there, and I love all the many sensations in that part of my body.

I love having my muscles massaged. Sometimes I forget, and it's remarkable how grand I can feel when someone else coaxes the stubborn ones to relax. My muscles love to tighten and relax, tighten and relax. I love the feeling of happy muscles.

My feet and my toes especially love to be massaged. My feet work so hard and are expected to carry my weight everywhere I want to go. I ask them to be prepared to do my bidding any time, and sometimes they just get so tired. They love to be treated to a loving touch. My individual toes love to be given special attention and are so happy when they get it. I love to make my feet and toes happy.

Sometimes, when I pay close attention, I can feel my heart beating and my blood pulsing in my veins. It is awesome that my heart works every moment of every day to keep me alive. I am very grateful to my heart, and I like doing everything I can to make it happy. I love my heart.

And I love the feelings I get in my heart area when I love anything. I love that feeling spreading throughout my whole body when I focus on that love. I feel very nurtured whenever I am in the space of love. It doesn't matter if it is me *loving something or someone else, or if I am the object of that love. The simple feeling of love is stunning. And being "in love" is perhaps the greatest feeling of all. I love* love, *and my body really loves* love.

Everything seems to go better for me when my body is happy. It is worth my time and effort to keep my body happy, and I do it with great joy. I love my body, and I'm honored and grateful that it loves me. My body is always my beloved friend.

If a man happens to find himself, he has a mansion which
he can inhabit with dignity all the days of his life.
James A. Michener

Chapter 11

Calling Every Part of Us to Come Home

Sometimes, in spite of all the work we have done to heal and master our lives, there seems to be something missing. Perhaps it shows itself as an inability to accomplish things or to perform as well as we know we can. Maybe there's a vague feeling or an unidentified sadness that threatens to overwhelm us. Possibly there is a recurring feeling that the joy of life is missing. Or, perhaps, there is a sense that there is something unforgivable or unacceptable about us, or a denial that some trait or behavior is a part of us. It could merely be an indefinable hunger for something not clearly seen and almost familiar, but not quite.

In shamanic terms, these would be called symptoms of soul loss. In more psychological terms they could be symptoms of some dissociative disorder. However we describe this experience, if we are to look at it from an empowered perspective we need to see ourselves as the active agent. That is, we have done something to ourselves, likely for very good reasons. I'm going to talk about these experiences in shamanic terms because that is the most empowered approach that I know of.

So, why do we lose pieces of ourselves? The most obvious answer is shame. Earlier in this book, we defined shame as the choice to disapprove of some aspect of who we are. This entire book is about overcoming shame and coming back to approving of ourselves. But there are lots of times in our lives when we haven't had the tools, the time, the understanding, or the safety to deal with challenges to our self-love. If we can't figure out how to safely accommodate aspects of ourselves in a situation (family, school, work, etc.), we most likely can only handle it by denying that part of us. Out of necessity, we have to pretend that we are other than we know ourselves to be.

The most important consideration is to be exceedingly kind and compassionate with ourselves. We have parts of our personality that have been very afraid to show themselves. We want them to return; we can't be whole beings without them. But we have to be incredibly gentle with them. They are likely to be very fragile.

This need for kindness and gentleness is also true for those pieces of ourselves that we can't face that are just too overwhelmingly big in terms of emotional impact. Experiences of abuse, horror, terror, guilt, or significant loss can generate the need to push pieces of ourselves away. The intensity was much too great to deal with it at that time. We can never be fully present to ourselves until we have felt all the way through these experiences. But getting to that point may seem impossible.

Another way we lose pieces of ourselves is when we have seemingly given our power away. We might have submitted our authority to someone who has or had some fundamental control over us. We might have had to do that to feel loved or approved of. We might have had to do that for financial reasons or coercion. Or we might have had to do it for physical or emotional survival.

If we are to successfully reintegrate these pieces into ourselves, and that may not always be possible, we need to remember that we are the ones who sent these pieces away. This is not about finding who to blame or to absolve anyone's inappropriate behavior. It is about recognizing that only in taking back our power, as we explored in Chapter 9, can we create the lives we want.

We are not victims in this. We probably had excellent reasons to push these pieces away at the time. We were likely trying to solve a significant problem by doing so. But now it's time to bring them back.

I suggest that as you read this chapter, you begin to invite your missing pieces to return. You don't have to do anything right now. Just be willing to go through the process of having these pieces come back home. This is a relatively straightforward process, but it might seem daunting. Remember, your feelings can't hurt you, but resisting them can.

Before I go through the steps in this process of reclaiming our pieces, I want to be explicit about the assumptions I have. We are created by some Consciousness that didn't make us flawed or with extraneous parts. We are intended to be whole creatures, here to explore what it means to be a human being. There are challenges in life, and we get to learn from them. But at no time are any aspects of our being bad, wrong, or evil. We are simply learning how to love better each and every day, as best we can.

Another way of looking at the same thing is to see ourselves as great beings who have tightened up and restricted our inner world in order to survive. This feels like a great clench. We choke off aspects of ourselves that don't seem to fit in. What is called the "false self" or "the ego" in other cultures and systems is merely the part of us that is left after the choking off.

From this perspective, what we so often don't like about ourselves—our greediness, neediness, and our need to make ourselves seem more significant than we really are—are what remains of us after trying to make our way safely in this world. When we have cut off all the natural ways that we have to feel good and to feel good about ourselves, we are left with a desperate struggle to be whole without any possible way to do so.

From this angle, the way back home is to intentionally open ourselves up, particularly when it feels uncomfortable or scary. This is a very courageous path and may not be possible for everyone. But having more than one perspective gives us a way to more easily understand what we're dealing with.

It's important to remember at this point what we want to do. We are returning to our power and our ability to determine how we want to live our lives. A self-empowered or self-realized person has his or her own sense of who they are. They don't get their identity by relying on other people's ideas or feelings. A self-empowered person discovers it within themselves. This is a continuing practice, as that sense of identity changes over time, naturally. But it also changes as we deny or embrace aspects of ourselves. The self-realized person is a whole being who is conscious of him or herself.

And this is certainly more fun than hiding who we are!

To integrate these pieces, we need to change our identities a little to accommodate them. That is, as we bring in a lost piece, we must think of ourselves in a way that includes the returned portion. Otherwise, we are still not including it as a part of ourselves. This process is more than celebrating the return of a part of us, which is a worthy and necessary action by itself. It is making sure that we encompass the returned part in our thoughts about who we are.

It's like adopting a child. We certainly want to show our delight in our new family member, but we also want to introduce our new member to our friends and other family members. We make sure that the child, or the piece of us, knows that it is part of the family.

We redefine who we are by not only accepting the returned piece but also actively approving of it. It left because we disapproved of it in some way, whether that was because we couldn't handle the pain of facing it or we were too ashamed of it for some reason. If we only accept that piece but can't quite actually approve of it, then we are still disapproving of it and are still ashamed of that piece.

We need to modify our identities each day, by the thoughts we have when we look into the mirror, by the things we let go of in our life, by the new desires we have, and by our increased awareness of our environment.

There are five steps to this process:
    1) Find and identify a lost piece

2) Make sure that we are fully willing to accept this piece back
3) Make it safe to be who we are with the returned piece
4) Prepare a loving welcome
5) Identify with the returned piece as an essential part of our wholeness

Step 1: Find and identify a lost piece

We generally accept that the way things are right now is more or less how they're supposed to be. Certainly, some things are broken or hurt and need healing. But for the most part, the lives we live seem to be just the nature of living.

Suppose, however, that what we are aware of is but a small fraction of who we really are and what we can be. Suppose that if we could but look at ourselves from a much higher perspective, we could see ourselves in the context of something enormously more magnificent than the small lives we've been aware of, so far.

From this higher perspective we can see parts of us that we have been unconscious of for some time. We can see how useful it would be to reintegrate these pieces now that we have both survived the circumstances that led to their departure and learned how much we'd like to have them back again. Looking at these pieces from our ordinary perspective makes these pieces look foreign and mysterious. Looking at them from the higher perspective, they look like forgotten jewelry or clothes lost in the dim recesses of a closet.

These pieces of us were never really missing. We just didn't look for them, for whatever good reason we had. So to find these pieces we look for what's missing, what seems to be calling us, and what we're passionate about.

Very often we start from a place of numbness, a sense that we don't know which way to go or even that we don't want to go anywhere. That's the place that feels like soul loss. But soul loss is only a perspective. It's like an eclipse. The sun or the moon isn't actually gone; we just can't see them because other things are in the way. It's like the missing jewelry hidden by other things in the drawer.

So, when we say things like, "I can't do this" or "I can't be like that" or "It's impossible," we lose our ability to see the things we most desperately want to look at.

On the other hand, when we say things like "What did I give up to survive such-and-such?" and "What do I miss most in my life?" and "Who seems to be living the life I'd like to have?" we start to see glimpses of what we've let go of. Yes, we might have fears about reintegrating something that we were terrified of seeing, hearing, or feeling. But the first step is about at least saying to ourselves, "Okay, let's just see what this is!" It is an act of bravery that is the price we pay for becoming whole.

Step 2: Make sure that we are fully willing to accept this piece back.

Letting a piece come back into ourselves means that we must be willing to change who we are a little. We have to accept that we will be a bit different, both to ourselves and to those around us. That's something that happens every day whether we're aware of it or not. But these changes may be a little more significant than usual.

For instance, if I decide to feel the full impact of my parents' divorce when I was a young child, I may go through some periods of hurt, anger, or mistrust. These will pass as I get more used to the feelings, heal them, and integrate the whole experience into the rest of my experiences. But it might take a little while.

However, if I am afraid of looking at the pain and hurt I felt as a child in connection with that divorce, I will not feel safe to fully experience the return of that piece. We may have a fear of abandonment that needs to be addressed first, for instance. We may have to accept some things that have been uncomfortable in the past and perhaps are still uncomfortable today.

There is a certain courage that's called for now, and we may need to face some of the fears that led to our piece becoming estranged. We may feel a need to ask for forgiveness from this piece for abandoning it. However, forgiving ourselves for what we felt we had to do is part of taking responsibility for our lives and is a necessary act.

Step 3: Make it safe to be who we are with the returned piece

There are two parts to feeling it is safe to be who we are: the outer environment and our inner one.

The outer environment includes our physical safety, our financial security, and the possessions we care about. Most of us naturally want to live in relatively safe environments. It's not always possible, of course, but we do the best we can. When we are not physically safe we need to do whatever we can to stay as safe as possible, and that may include pretending to be other than we are.

To be safe in the inner environment, we need to be very clear that criticizing ourselves, judging ourselves, and shaming ourselves is not okay. We hate to feel bad about ourselves and will do almost anything to avoid those feelings, including hiding from them. Unfortunately, we often accept other people's ideas about how we should act and how we should be. If we don't measure up to the standards of these opinions, we start feeling shame.

The pieces that we are asking to return need to know that we will not make them feel bad. They left feeling bad; they need to know that they are genuinely welcome back.

Here's a short exercise to give you a sense of how you might regard these estranged pieces. Think of a child or small animal that you once held in your arms or hands. Visualize them right here and now. Feel how vulnerable they are. Feel how much they need your love and care. Feel how important gentleness and kindness are for them. Now, feel into your own body with that same love and care, and notice where in your body you feel it the most. Whether you were brought up to be tough and strong or not, allow yourself to be just as vulnerable and in need of love as the little child or animal you were just imagining. Let your body armor relax, and let go of your defenses. You can put them back on later if you want to. Right now, allow yourself to be loved and cared for. Gently and lovingly reassure yourself that everything is all right, and that you are here and always will be here to nurture and protect all aspects of your being.

Now, here are some ways to help you feel safe to be who you are: Choose to live in a place where people accept you as you are. Choose to stop hiding who you really are. Decide for yourself that who you are is entirely acceptable to you. Find a way to talk about yourself without any criticism at all. Aggressively counter any criticism from others—not with denial, but with an inner love, and reaffirm your self-acceptance. This is most easily done when you have become your own authority. Be willing to look at the things that you have felt shame about in your life. That means you look at the things you've done, you've felt, you've desired, as well as all parts of your body. They are all good if you will only look at them that way!

Step 4: Prepare a loving welcome

When you are bringing home pieces of yourself, some kind of welcoming ritual can help immensely. This is a way of integrating and celebrating who you are. Rituals could be as simple as having a nice dinner alone and being present to this newly incorporated piece. Or it could be a private dance of loving reunion. Or it could be some form of making love to this piece.

This welcoming ritual is best when it feels meaningful to you, and it lets your body know that you are genuinely glad to have this piece return. You want this to reflect the value of this piece to you and the honor and respect you have for it.

Step 5: Identify with the returned piece as an essential part of our wholeness

To integrate these pieces we need to change our identities to accommodate them. That is, as we bring in a lost part, we must now think of and feel about ourselves in a way that includes the returned piece. Otherwise, we are still keeping it outside of us.

We redefine who we are by accepting the returned piece and actively approving of it. This is the antidote to what drove the piece away in the first place. We stopped accepting that it was a part of us. Now is the time to recognize that we needed to let this piece go at the time, and that we are entirely ready to pull this piece back.

Here is a visualization to help you in asking your lost pieces to show themselves.

Picture yourself in a lovely garden. It could be a garden you've been in before, or it could be some garden that seems to be appearing for this exercise. Take some time and look at one thing in your garden very carefully, and notice as much as you can about this one thing. Then focus your attention on what you can hear in your garden and listen to one thing as carefully as you can. Then find something to touch in your garden and feel its texture, its flexibility, and its shape.

Now, somewhere in your garden find a comfortable place to build a campfire. You can put it together yourself, or just tell it to appear. And put seats of some sort around this nice campfire. Make it a warm, welcoming place.

Using your inner voice, loudly invite all your lost soul pieces to come and sit by the fire. Some may not want to get too close and may wish to remain somewhat hidden, and that's fine. All you want to do is let them reveal something about themselves and for you to recognize them. You can reintegrate them later, if they're ready. Right now, just see who comes; and let them show themselves as they feel more relaxed.

Make it as safe as possible for them, and be as warm and loving as you can. If these parts of you feel like talking, listen intently. Whatever they have to say is okay and safe to hear. There is nothing wrong with any of them.

You may find pieces spontaneously reintegrating, but you're more likely to need to do some more work. You may have to make some deal with them for them to be willing to return. This could be a promise never to shame them again. It might be a commitment to increase your level of intensity tolerance so that you can fully feel the experience that that piece underwent. It could be a pledge to be the sovereign of your own being and never again let anyone control you. Let this be a loving negotiation for the benefit of all concerned.

Allow your gathering to continue until you feel that you've done all that you can at this time. At some point, you will likely have a sense that it is complete. Be sure to thank all the pieces that have come, even the ones that weren't ready to reintegrate. Every bit of you needs to know that they are loved, no matter what!

The Party of Integration

You can just read this visualization and feel the power of it. You could record it to listen to later. Or you could get someone to read it to you, slowly, so that you can feel the intensity of the experience.

There are four parts of a party: Inviting everyone, getting all the supplies in and cleaning up for it, the gathering itself and enjoying one another, and the aftermath. For this party, invite all the parts of yourself to come. Think of all the areas of your life, all the different things you do, want to do, and remember doing. Think of the different kinds of experiences you have in your life: eating, sex, fantasies, the different relationships and different types of relationships you have, your work, and your hobbies. Think of all of the various stages of *you* in life—you as a baby, a child, a teenager, a young adult, a middle-aged person, an elder, getting ready to die. Think of you cleaning your environment, bathing, driving, your sense of the divine, your experiences of transcendence. You are a different person in each of these areas.

So, invite every one of the pieces of yourself. Most especially, invite all the parts of you that you are uncomfortable with and all those pieces that you have abandoned at any time. At this point you don't have to fix anything, just acknowledge their presence and let them know that you want them to come to the party.

Now clean the space, your heart space, in preparation for the party. Sweep out any judgments or criticisms. Vacuum up any residual angers, grievances, or resentments. Open the windows and let a fresh breeze of acceptance blow in.

Prepare a great table of wonderful things to feast on. If it were me, I'd put out big mounds of light and airy joy, long cakes of deep satisfaction, shimmering bowls of jolliness, steaming tureens of sweet comfort, and great platters of delicate kindnesses. I'd put out fat dumplings of generosity, grand salads of sacred acceptance, frothy fountains of fun, and big ornate bowls overflowing with beauty. I'd make a place for assorted tartlets of curiosity, wonder, and awe, juicy berries of bliss with cream and sugar, sweet-scented pâtés of compassion and care, savory stews of success and service, and baskets of benevolence. I'd prepare fine noodles of connection, spicy sauces of passion and excitement, rich bars of wisdom and discernment, and long, long kebobs of friendship. I'd serve luscious pastries filled with patience and empathy, great trays of insight and understanding, enormous casks of cool forgiveness, fragrant pies of delight and pleasure, and tubs and tubs of laughter and giggles. Use your imagination and serve what inspires *you*!

It's time now for the party to begin. Once all the guests have arrived your job is to introduce each guest to all the others. Help them get to know one another. Deal with any friction with an immediate dose of forgiveness, as large as is necessary to return to harmony. And don't forget to have fun yourself. Enjoying your party and each guest is essential to everyone else enjoying it. This is a time to celebrate all the glorious aspects of who you are. It is a time for the divinity in you to see the divinity in you. Namaste.

As the party progresses, you may notice that some of the guests are melding into one another. Somehow they are coming into each other and losing their separateness. Watch with appreciation and love as your guests, the various parts of you, lose their individuality and begin to come together as a harmonious whole. And if any parts still seem to stand apart you can gently help to bring them into yourself. Bring them all into yourself with gentle peace and care.

And when you are the only one left, take some time to see how you feel. With a party like this, there's no mess, just good residual feelings. Savor these feelings and count your blessings. Give thanks for all that you are. Give thanks to all the magnificent aspects of your whole, authentic self. You are a wondrous, beautiful being, aren't you?

Home is where the whole family can feel safe and valued. We call all of the facets of our being back to where they are loved and cherished. It is from this place that we can authentically create the world we want to inhabit. Without being whole, our creations are incomplete and crippled. We can't see the entire picture of our lives, and thus we are hampered in responding to our inner callings. We come home so that we can explore the even greater parts of our being.

Meditation 11
Befriending Myself

Sometimes I feel like I am all alone in this world. I feel disconnected from the people around me, and I don't sense that others particularly care about me. I know in my head that there are people who care for me, but sometimes I can't feel that in my heart.

In my heart, I want to feel that I am connected—connected to other people, connected to love, connected to life itself. I want to feel that delicious feeling of being loved.

Perhaps I can feel loved without relying on others to make me feel that way. Perhaps I can find that love within. Perhaps I can love myself the way I deeply wish to be loved.

It's okay if I feel lonely. It's okay if I want more love in my life. It's okay that I want to feel alive and joyous. I just need to be open to feeling.

When I relax, I can enjoy hearing the birds singing. When I relax, I can appreciate the beauty of flowers and leaves. When I relax, I can enjoy the beauty of works of art and music. When I relax, I can enjoy the wonderful gems of life. And I feel good.

I can feel good about the things around me that I like whenever I give them my attention. I can feel good about the people I care about whenever I give them my attention. By changing my focus, I can feel good about lots of things.

If I were my own best friend what would I be like? Would I be kind to myself? Or would I constantly criticize myself? Would I go walking with myself or would I stay at home, putting myself down? Would I focus on my faults or would I appreciate the things about me that I like?

Is it safe for me to be my friend? Is it safe for me to be who I am? I think so. I think it is safe to be my own friend. And it is safe to be me.

As I look within myself, I can see a truly beautiful person. Sometimes I am hidden by all the things I think I could do better. But I don't need to be better right now. I will simply enjoy this beautiful person that lives inside of me.

To be a good friend to myself, I look for things to compliment. I spend time with myself, just enjoying my company. I make it a point to simply be present to myself, and to listen to all I have to say, to listen to what I am feeling, and to hear the love in my voice as I talk about my life.

As a friend, I am just fine the way I am. I don't have to change a thing to be my friend. I let myself be who I am, and I let myself do those things that I like to do. I treat myself just as nicely and as compassionately as I treat any other dear friend.

The one I want to love me the most is me. I can love myself best by being a good friend. Each day now I show myself what a good friend I am. Just like I want my other friends to feel that I love them, I want myself to feel that I love me.

Today I am a good friend to myself. Tomorrow I will still be a good friend.

Thank you, my dear friend!

*A friend told me that each morning when we get up we have to decide
whether we are going to save or savor the world.
I don't think that is the decision. It's not an either-or, save or savor.
We have to do both, save and savor the world.*
Kate Clinton

Chapter 12

Sharing the Peace

We come home to find the peace within us. This is the precious treasure that awaits us when we stop hurting ourselves, and we summon the courage to accept all of what we are. This prize is available to all of us. While to claim it does require that we change some of our habits and experience the pain we've hidden from, it rewards each effort with an increase in pleasure and joy. Every time we let go of a criticism or complaint and appreciate something it increases our well-being. Each story that we change from victimhood to triumph adds to our happiness. All the expectations that we own and use with expertise contribute to our sense of wholeness and integrity. When we're mindful of what we are doing, we find our way back to the most magnificent lives imaginable.

It's from this point that we can best create the life that satisfies our hearts and souls. There are a great many ways that being at home presents itself. Being present to oneself and whatever else that is right there, a sweet pervasive kindness, exhibiting a generosity of spirit and humor, and gentle playfulness are significant signs of being at home. A balance between the inner world and the outer one, a reverence for all life, and abundant friendships are sure indications. Persistent gratitude, frequently savoring of all the joys of the senses and heart, and acceptance of whatever has gone before are also marks of that place. Actively choosing new things to explore and enjoy, and choosing the best for everyone—including oneself—are also emblematic.

Some other factors are also important. Coming home to ourselves is the first step in coming home to our planet. It is classic wisdom: As within, so without. We won't be able to effectively change how we humans deal with the Earth and each other until we can successfully change how we deal with ourselves. Fighting for peace just doesn't work. Greed will never produce abundance for all. Discord between us never resolves itself into harmony. Disrespect for others in any way can only come from disrespecting ourselves. And the idealistic or Utopian ideas can never be approached without embodying them first.

If we are ever to create a world where we can all be at home, we need to start with a strong foundation. We can't build a home for humanity, and all life, without first making sure that we are beginning from stable and solid building blocks. Let's remember that *we* are those building blocks.

Just as we had to believe that it was possible for us to change, to do things differently, and to come home to ourselves, we must believe that a world that cares for all life is possible and desirable. And the place to start is with ourselves. If we're not tranquil within ourselves, how can we possibly create tranquility in our outer world? If we can't be comfortable in ourselves, how can we ever craft a world where all beings can be comfortable?

Staying at Home

There is a tricky point that we need to be aware of as we live in the cultures that we do. We naturally care about many things: our families, our friends and neighbors, our town or city, our country, the people of this world, and the Earth itself. To not care about any of these is to miss the beauty and excitement of living.

Some may call this attachment and, of course, it is. The argument against attachment is based on the presumption of suffering when something changes regarding the object of our attachment. When things or circumstances change, our relationships change as well, and we can't stay attached in the way we have been. This can easily lead to disappointment. But, as we have seen, the suffering of disappointment, or any variant of it, is a choice. We can make other choices if we want to.

By being attached to something we often get assaulted by bad news or challenges to the well-being of that to which we're attached. If something happens to a member of our family, or if our neighborhood is threatened, we naturally want to do something about that.

The tricky point I mentioned is wanting to help without being lured out of our place of being at home within ourselves. If we get angry, we're wandering into the wilderness again. If we get sad, our focus is on something in the past or something we imagine will happen in the future, not on what is in the present moment. To get upset is quite literally to upset our own well-being. So how can we care about these things without kicking ourselves back out of home?

The trick is to remind ourselves of who we are and to stay in the awareness of our own existence. It is so very important that we continue to trust ourselves. Remember the powers of pleasure? We are much more effective in whatever we do when we feel good inside ourselves. It takes a certain amount of self-confidence to maintain equilibrium inside ourselves while dealing with important things outside. That takes practice and comes over time with intention and awareness. But it is imperative to maintain it.

The more one gets to know one's self, whether through therapy, meditation, prolonged quiet time, or general introspection, the easier it is for them to find their way home again after inadvertently stepping away from it. We have to decide how much distress we are willing to endure before we choose to care in a different way.

It's not that we don't care, or we don't care enough. We need to care within the context of our own lives and the well-being of us and those around us. When the feeling of pain or grief overwhelms our ability to stay centered, we have moved out of the place where we can be most effective and strong.

For some people, the measure of caring is how upset we get. That's like saying that the measure of love is in how jealous we get. Being upset or jealous has nothing to do with how much we care; those things are measures of how much our fears control us. If we look, we can find a place of balance that lets us help when we can, but not to our own detriment.

Once we have found our way back to the home we have inside us, we want to stay there as much as possible. There really isn't anything that is worth giving up that centeredness for. Everything that we can do can come from that place. And there is a lot more in the way of spiritual knowledge, psychic wisdom, intuition, and personal power that can only come from being in that space.

Dealing with Injustice

I need to speak in personal terms here to convey these ideas without generalizing too much. I am very passionate about injustice, and I need to recognize that others have different passions and that mine is one of many.

I found myself getting angry in the wee hours of the morning recently, waking me up from a deep sleep. I was angry with the craziness that my country seems to have embraced now. I was angry at the vast economic inequities in the United States and its effects on so many millions of people. I was angry at the pollution that is ignored in favor of making more weapons and profits. I was angry at the hate for people who are different. When I let myself look at the reasons for my anger, there were lots of things in the world that I'm angry about.

These feelings of anger aren't a part of how I see myself. For the most part, I have released the angers of the past. I have gotten over the various kinds of expectations and all the disappointments that seem to follow expectations. I know better than to blame others for how I feel. I give people permission to be who they are and to do what they do.

Yet these angers persist. They are the angers at injustice, insensitivity, and, yes, stupidity. I have resisted giving these feelings too much awareness, choosing to focus on the beauty in the world and all the joy that surrounds me. I highly prize the highest vibrations I can achieve and strongly oppose those feelings that bring me down. I believe that maintaining as high a vibration as I can muster is one way I can be of service in this world. Being in a place of anger, resentment, or outrage only adds more negative vibration to what there is already too much of.

Forgiveness isn't enough in this case. I can keep forgiving and more or less bring myself back to being centered, but not quite. I can forgive myself for my contributions to the situation, even if I'm not sure what they were. I can forgive other people for not seeing things the way I see them and for making choices that I would be embarrassed by. But still, it's not enough.

There remain a great many things that I cannot condone and that seem to create massive but entirely unnecessary suffering. What, then, do I do with all those feelings?

When I allow my feelings to get as big as they need to and then subside, I remember that I am not here on Earth to solve all the world's problems. I need to save a few for others to solve. I do need to do something. And that's the key here. I am angry in large part at my own impotence. Compassion prompts me to want to help, but I can't fix the problem.

However, I can always do *something*. If nothing else, I can send healing energy (whatever that seems to be at the time) to all those who I learn are suffering. I have friends who do this with each newspaper article they read that provokes compassion. I can write letters to those whose job it is to remedy situations that I think need fixing. I can help bring awareness of issues to those who want to hear what I have to say. I can volunteer for some things that can have a direct impact on other people's lives.

The point is that there are things to be done as quickly as possible while we get back into the higher vibration. Letting go of the anger is the critical part. If we do that best by actively doing something, that's great. If we can do that by changing our vibration with our thoughts and feelings, that's wonderful, too. But I know for myself that I have to allow that anger to show itself fully and to address it in some way before I can send heavy-duty, loving energy abroad.

Anger serves us by inciting us to act. It will make us sick, though, if it stays with us for long. And that serves no one. By returning to our center as quickly as possible while making some substantial contribution to the world, we balance ourselves in this life that we love so much.

For me, there's an excellent little formula for this: Feel, act, love. Repeat. That is, fully feel my anger so that I'm not repressing any of it. Then find something, anything, that feels like I'm doing something to help solve the problem or to rectify the situation *to some degree*. This doesn't mean taking responsibility for the solution. It does mean contributing to the solution.

Then it's time to move back into my joy vibration. I know I am most effective when I am in that space. I am most powerful when my energy is high. Whether that is just helping my mind think better or sharing that high vibration with others, it affects the world. And I stay there until I feel enough pressure from the things that I don't like to go through the process again. I do what I can, and make sure that I remember that that's enough. Trying to do more will only weaken me and make me less productive overall.

I find that it is an interesting balance between reacting to the world and taking good care of myself. Both impulses need to be in harmony. If we forget that, we have lost it all.

Dealing with Those Who Hurt Others

Most of us start with what we need to survive: food, water, shelter, and sleep. We want these things at the deepest levels of our being, and we will work very hard to get them. And when we do get them, there is a definite pleasure in having them. Even if the food isn't very good, we get pleasure from it if we're very hungry. We're always trying to feel better.

But what about those people who do acts of significant harm to others? These people seem to find joy in harming other beings.

We're dealing with hypothetical situations here, and we need to be careful about what we are assuming. We can't assume that people are acting in a vacuum or without some context. The sadistic person has his or her pleasures based on *feeling better*, just like the rest of us. We don't know what they were feeling before their acts of cruelty. We don't even know for sure what they were feeling during those acts or even if they were feeling anything. But let's assume that they were acting in a way that felt better than what they were feeling before.

Perhaps they chronically felt unloved, weak, and depressed. Being cruel to others could be a way of feeling a little more powerful, even if it's a false power and very temporary. It still feels better than feeling unloved, weak, and hopeless—probably a lot better. Are there other feelings that would work a great deal better? Most certainly! But those better feelings may not be accessible to someone who thinks that they deserve to be punished or that they are fundamentally unworthy. Judging other people's motivations can lead us into a kind of thinking that is more about us and our own fears, than about the other person.

It's important to remember that not all feelings are great ones, and they don't need to be to be quite valid. Anger and rage are considered to be negative emotions. But, like most things in life, they are positive or negative depending on how we view them. Anger and rage are a lot better than depression and numbed endurance. Pessimism feels better than anger. Hope feels better than pessimism. Positive expectation feels better than hope. And joy feels better than positive expectation.

When we talk about pleasure, we're talking about feeling better in a moment *relative* to what was being felt before that moment.

Hope, then, is a pleasure when it follows anger, but is less pleasurable when it follows joy.

We can be more compassionate toward others when we look at their motivations, knowing that they are trying to feel better than how they have been feeling. We can act on that compassion; not by condemning their feelings, but by recognizing their motivations and steering their actions toward more life-affirming paths, if we can.

We need to make a distinction between what someone is feeling and how he or she is acting. There are a great many laws that provide sanctions against people who harm others. We need to have these laws for a sane and orderly society. However, we also need to accept someone's pain and their attempts to feel better. Accepting their feelings without accepting their behavior is a good place to start.

When we tell someone that their anger is wrong, we prevent them from using their own inner wisdom to seek to feel better. All we are doing is encouraging them to feel bad about themselves. This is counterproductive and a net loss of joy in the world. When we recognize that their anger feels better than their suffering, we begin the process of getting to even better feelings. We might go from anger to thoughts about revenge. Revenge feels better than anger, but carries significant penalties. A feeling somewhat higher on the scale might work better, like expressing the anger in some constructive context, as in deciding to never be in the same situation again. Forgiveness, better yet, is a feeling that will come along at the point where the anger is no longer important.

The critical thing to remember here is that we don't have to like someone's actions when they hurt others. By helping them to deal with their feelings, if we can, we can sometimes change a situation of rage and hurt into one of understanding and peace.

There was a marvelous story in the news some years back about an excessively abusive man on a commuter train in Japan. He was raging against everyone near him, even striking those who got too close. Another commuter dared to go up to him and, speaking gently and kindly, asked him about his troubles. Little by little, the wild commuter relaxed and talked about the terrible things that had just happened to him at work and at home. Eventually, he calmed down and started to cry on the brave fellow commuter's shoulder, and the rest of the commute was peaceful.

We can't always help like that, but there are more instances than we might suspect where we could recognize that someone who is hurting others is in pain, and we can help more with understanding than with anger or demands for "justice." A little love in the face of ugliness and fear can go a long way!

The essence of all real pleasure is self-love

In the course of coming home and learning how to be kind and compassionate to ourselves, one vital element is that of savoring the peace and serenity that we have journeyed so far to find. It's such a wonderful feeling that we want to wrap ourselves in it as much as possible. But it's just like any other wonderful feeling as the intensity of the feeling grows when we hold our attention on it.

The process of savoring, taking the time to enjoy something thoroughly, is a sacred art that is a non-intellectual way of connecting to the transcendent. By simply feeling the depth of pleasure about anything, we open to that higher part of ourselves that is connected to all.

However, savoring intensely can be daunting. Fully savoring, that is, feeling that pleasure throughout our entire body, means that we are aware of the core of our being as well. If we haven't fully accepted who we are, as is the case with most of us, then it can be hard to look at ourselves fully and see all the things we've been resisting all these years.

Savoring can be a practice, a form of yoga, where we incrementally open ourselves more and more into the greatness of our being. Savoring breakfast is an excellent start. Savoring the work we do is also a good one. And then savoring the huge stuff, the stuff that is the most beautiful aspect of our lives, like love and happiness, takes patience and practice. But, oh my, it is so worth it!

I worked with a man not long ago in a workshop where he revealed that he couldn't find his passion and that all the lovely things I was saying about feeling the great things in life didn't resonate at all in his body. He was clearly a very intelligent man who didn't express any great traumas or severe blockages to life. He just didn't feel much and didn't know how to go about doing so.

I had been pointing out that all the great things in life—love, peace, happiness, harmony, joy, compassion, to name a few—are all feelings. This discussion was in the context of manifestation, and I also pointed out that there were one or more feelings that were desired underlying everything anyone wanted to manifest.

What may fairly be obvious is that each of these feelings is intense. We have to be willing to experience great intensity to swim in these wonderful feelings. But the not-so-obvious aspect is that to feel the intensity of beautiful feelings we have to be willing to feel the intensity of **all** of our feelings. If we only are willing to feel the good stuff, we are limited in our ability to feel in general. It works a great deal like sliding doors, like the ones on elevators and subway cars do. When one side opens, the other side opens equally. They work in tandem.

When we open ourselves to the full range of feelings, we are able to feel the full intensity of the feelings we like. That naturally means being willing to feel all the yucky stuff as well as the cool stuff. Being willing to feel the pains, the hurts, the angers, and all the other scary feelings doesn't mean we have to hang out with them. We merely need to be willing to feel them enough to heal them before intentionally turning our focus to the feelings we prefer.

The man I was dealing with in the workshop was very careful to only allow the good feelings into his life and wondered why he didn't feel them very intensely. When I pointed out the nature of intensity and its sliding door aspects he understood that to feel the passion, a very intense feeling, he would need to open himself to all his feelings. He was a little disappointed that I couldn't just fix it so that he could only feel what he wanted to and not deal with the difficult stuff. But he was smart enough to understand that he could go where he wanted to just by opening more fully to his feelings in general.

Savoring, then, is more than just taking the time to enjoy one thing thoroughly. It is also the expansion of our ability to feel more fully. It is the gradual breaking down of our resistance to ourselves and to life. It is a practice that takes us step-by-step toward our own self-realization.

How do we come home to ourselves? Practice, practice, practice!

Alan Cohen wrote an excellent book called *Joy Is My Compass* and talked about recognizing that by following joy he could live a spectacularly wonderful life. I find it fascinating that so many people declare that they want joy, but rather than simply enjoying the present moment they spend their time preparing to enjoy a future moment. It's like the old cartoon showing a hallway with two doors, the one saying "Heaven Here," and the other saying "The Workshop for Getting into Heaven." We can go there now, or we can perpetually prepare for it.

Joy, pleasure, happiness, feeling good, whatever you want to call it, is not a logical outcome of anything. It is a choice to experience it whenever possible. However, it's also important to note that feeling good is how we recognize health and how we recognize that we are in harmony with the world around us and with our inner being. As we grow up and grow into the fullness of who we are, we can easily see whether or not we are working towards our greater good. We can feel it when we pay attention. What many of us do is fail to trust that sense of feeling good. We create a huge array of appropriate patterns, templates, and rules about how we should be developing, often overriding the built-in guidance system we all have.

The great endpoints, the culmination of years of practice, meditation, and prayer of the world's various spiritual paths, are all about being in a place or state of feeling incredibly good. They, of course, would have no adherents if they didn't promise extraordinary feelings. The unspeakable joys of coming home, of heaven, the bliss of enlightenment, the ecstasies of paradise, all speak to the supremacy of feeling as the essential purpose of life. It does not make any sense, then, to try to think our way to these states. The "logical" thing to do is to feel—not just a little, but as much as possible. It's much like the directions to Carnegie Hall. How do you get home? Practice, practice, practice.

This is not just about enjoying the things that present themselves to our awareness. It is about actively looking for the pleasure and joy in whatever life shows us. It's like the classic Zen story about the Zen Master and the tiger. The Master was walking along a path when a man-eating tiger spotted him and ran toward him. In his effort to get away, the Master ran over to the nearby cliff, grabbed hold of a vine dangling over the cliff, and clambered down out of reach of the hungry tiger. He looked down and there, far below, were sharp rocks that would mean death were he to fall. Just then, two mice noticed the vine and started to eat it. As it became more evident that his demise was imminent, he noticed a single ripe strawberry growing on the side of the cliff within reach. With one hand on the vine, he reached over and plucked the strawberry. Popping it into his mouth, he exclaimed, "What a delicious strawberry!"

While we are not often confronted with such dire situations, we are regularly presented with options for our attention. Will we choose the worry, doubt, or fear? Or will we look for what will make us feel good at that moment? If we keep asking the question, "Where's the pleasure here?" we move into a focus on the elements of heaven in our everyday life.

Remember the connoisseurs of feelings? When we decide that we want to feel as good as possible we become more discerning about what we are currently exploring. "Is this feeling that I am experiencing right now good enough for me?" "What can I do to get to a superior feeling?" These are questions that lead us into higher and higher realms of consciousness.

Learning to trust feeling good may take some doing, especially if one is heavily invested in ideas about how things should be. But a healthy dose of skepticism and a willingness to experiment should show that feeling good works better than anything else to bring one into harmony with the Universe. This is the practice that is the essence of happiness. It is in exercising this muscle of focus that we can steer our lives toward our joy.

It takes a little effort to let the urgent things that don't matter go. And it takes a bit more effort to work our way through the deep fears that hide the joy that lives behind them. However, when we keep our aim on feeling good, rather than fulfilling some notion of duty, niceness, or correct behavior, we become good at stepping into heaven.

As Voltaire so nicely said, "Pleasure is the object, duty, and the goal of all rational creatures." Hear! Hear!

We have looked at how we might change our habits of hurting ourselves through criticism, worry, and regret. We've scanned the nature of expectations and the stories we tell about ourselves. And we've spent some time remembering to be kind and compassionate to ourselves. Now, let us all find the courage to come home to ourselves. We will be happier for it, and the world around us will share in that happiness.

Dear Reader,

Thank you for purchasing *It's Time to Come Home: With Kindness and Compassion We Come Back to Ourselves*. I hope you've enjoyed reading it and have found the ideas and perspectives helpful. But this isn't the end of the journey. I invite you to connect with me, and others who are on similar paths in other ways and places.

I welcome your feedback and questions at any time via email: shamanofpleasure@gmail.com. I will respond as quickly as I can and there is no charge for this. If you are interested in more extensive work with me, private sessions are available via telephone or Skype. Email me with what you are looking for and I will send you my rates. There are discounts available as needed.

You are also invited to join the *It's Time to Come Home* group on Facebook. This is a closed group for those who want to discuss the ideas and perspectives of this book with other people. Just ask to be a member. I contribute to this group regularly, but other members are invited to post there as well. My intention is for this to be a support group for those taking this courageous journey.

It would be a great service to me and to potential readers of this book if you would leave a review on Amazon.com. Your insights can be very useful for people considering purchasing this book. Thank you.

There are a lot more writings and information on my website: www.stewartblackburn.com. Please sign up there for *The Pleasure Journal* if you have an interest in receiving my blog.

And please don't forget that my first book, *The Skills of Pleasure*, is a valuable resource for those looking for more in life. Also available on Amazon.com.

I wish you great joy and peace in your trek to come home to yourself. May you find the kindness and compassion within to treat yourself as your beloved!

Fondly,
Stewart Blackburn

It's Time to Come Home

I, not events, have the power to make me happy or unhappy today. I can choose which it shall be. Yesterday is dead, tomorrow hasn't arrived yet. I have just one day, today, and I'm going to be happy in it.
Groucho Marx

Author Bio

Stewart Blackburn is a writer and teacher whose focus is on helping and encouraging people's journey home to themselves. He is the author of *The Skills of Pleasure: Crafting the Life You Want; It's Time to Come Home: With Kindness and Compassion, We Come Back to Ourselves,* and dozens of articles on shamanism, pleasure, and consciousness. He maintains a healing and teaching practice at his home in the jungle on the island of Hawaii.

Stewart is a trained professional chef with a Master's Degree in Food Science who has transitioned into a teacher, counselor, and mentor to those seeking more peace in their inner world. He draws upon his extensive studies of tantra, Buddhism, the mystical paths of the world, and wisdom from anywhere else that resonates with him.

Printed in Great Britain
by Amazon